Teacher's Book
Stages 1 & 2

English in a quarter of the time!

The Callan ® Method was first developed and published
in 1960 by R.K. T. Callan.
This edition was published for the international market in 2012.

Copyright © R.K.T. Callan 2012

Teacher's Book – Stages 1&2
ISBN 978-1-908954-00-8

CALLAN and the CALLAN logo are registered trade marks
of Callan Works Limited, used under licence by Callan Publishing Limited

Printed in the EU

Published by

CALLAN PUBLISHING LTD.
Orchard House, 45-47 Mill Way, Grantchester, Cambridge CB3 9ND
in association with CALLAN METHOD ORGANISATION LTD.

www.callan.co.uk

Introduction to Stages 1 and 2

The information below relates to Stages 1 and 2 only. For an explanation of how to conduct a Callan Method lesson, please read the Teacher's Handbook. Information on Callan Method training courses for teachers can be found by visiting the Callan Method website at www.callan.co.uk

Stages 1 and 2 are the beginner and post-beginner stages of the method. They introduce vital building blocks, such as the verbs "be" and "have", the present simple and present continuous, subject and object pronouns, and much indispensable vocabulary. These constitute the essential foundations for learning that follows at higher levels, and so progress through Stages 1 and 2 should not be rushed. Revision is exceptionally important at these low levels so that the student develops the ability to use structures and vocabulary without thinking. If these foundations are strong, progress will be better later on. If not, it will suffer.

Make sure new students know what to expect before their first lesson. As they are new to the Callan Method, the question-answer format, speed, error correction, and the sheer pace of the Callan Method will probably be very different from any language lessons they may have experienced before. Especially as regards error correction, students need to realize that you will correct their mistakes from the very start, that the correction will be instantaneous, that it is part of the method, and that it is for their benefit and an essential part of the learning process. This, along with everything they need to know about the method, is explained very clearly in the preface to the Student's Book, but an explanation and demonstration from you, their teacher, will be very useful.

Resist the temptation to speak more slowly during low-level classes. Right from the start, the student needs to start developing an ability to understand without translating; this is vital. As such, you should speak at the same brisk pace as you would with a high-level class. The student will get ample support from you through the repetition of the question, the initial prompt, the constant feeding of the answer, and the correction. Also bear in mind that material that may be difficult at first will be covered again and again in revision lessons.

Both Stages 1 and 2 contain numerous notes for the teacher. These notes are in small non-bold print and are there to give you essential instructions and also guide you in the early stages. It is important to read these carefully. Alongside these teacher notes, you will also see sections of text in slightly larger bold print. These must be read out to your class when you are introducing the material as new work. They are, in the main, explanations for the grammar or vocabulary that you are teaching, and the text often reappears in the answers to the questions that follow.

Instructions for students to do revision exercises start to appear at the end of Stage 1. The exercises themselves are only in the Student's Book as they are intended to be extra revision work that the student can do outside school. However, as you pass each instruction in the Teacher's Book, it is a good idea to remind your students that they are now ready for that particular exercise.

Always make sure you have the Callan Demonstration Chart with you. Whilst teaching Stages 1 and 2, you will often need to refer to the Demonstration Chart. There are icons placed throughout the Teacher's Book that flag up where it is required and which particular chart is needed.

Do a complete revision at the end of Stage 1 and Stage 2. At the end of Stage 1, you should do a complete revision of Stage 1 before starting Stage 2. Also, at the end of Stage 2, you should do a complete revision of both Stage 1 and Stage 2.

At the end of each stage, there is a Stage Exam. This can be used to check the progress of students before they move on to the next stage. More information can be found at the end of this book.

STAGE 1

LESSON 1

Pick up a pen, a pencil and a book one after the other, and, as you show each one in turn to the students, say

pen   **pencil**   **book**   **a**

Repeat these words about two or three times depending on the kind of students you have; that is, whether they are complete beginners, fast or slow, old or young, or whether the class is large or small.

what is (what's)   **this**   **it is (it's)**

Pick up the pen again, and say **What's this?** and then translate the question into the students' own language, explaining that "What's" is the contraction of "What is" and "It's" is the contraction of "It is" and that contractions are formed with an apostrophe. Then answer the question yourself by saying **It's a pen**, and again translate. You may have to do this two or three times, and again a few minutes later, to make it quite clear to the students what is meant. Next, turn to one of the students, and ask

What's this?   It's a pen

Repeat the above question for all three objects until the students answer without hesitation. Then continue in the same way with the remaining twelve objects. Take three at a time, and point to them carefully and forcefully, or pick them up, as the case may be, so that the student is in no doubt as to which object is intended. Time is wasted walking around touching the objects; the students will understand what you mean, even if, being at a distance, the word "that" should be used instead of "this". When you come to the word "room", look around you, and, at the same time, describe a large horizontal circle with your index finger. All such actions help. For the sake of simplicity, you can, for the moment, call your desk or the student's desk a table.

 *See Chart 1* (at the end of this book)

table	**chair**	**light**	**wall**
floor	**room**	**ceiling**	**window**
door	**clock**	**box**	**picture**
is this?		**yes**	

Pick up the pen and ask **Is this a pen?** and translate. Then answer **Yes, it's a pen** and translate. When you ask the question, raise your voice a little at the end. When you say "Yes", nod your head very emphatically. Then turn to the student and ask

Is this a pen?

Yes, it's a pen

Continue this kind of question with all the other objects the students have just learnt. If the students are quick, ask the questions very quickly towards the end of the list.

no, it is not (isn't)

Pick up a pen and ask **Is this a pen?** The student will naturally answer **Yes, it's a pen**. Then pick up a pencil, and ask **Is this a pen?** Then say **No, it isn't a pen; it's a pencil** and translate. When saying "No, it isn't", shake your head emphatically. Ask this kind of question for all the objects, making the last word of the student's answer the object in your next question, e.g. "Is this a pen?" "No, it isn't a pen; it's a pencil". Then, picking up the book, ask "Is this a pencil?" etc. It is important that the student answers in the full-length form, i.e. "No, it isn't a pencil; it's a book ".

Is this a pen?

No, it isn't a pen; it's a pencil

Is this a pencil?

No, it isn't a pencil; it's a book

 *See Chart 1*

long   short   the   contraction

For the words "long" and "short" point to the long pen and short pencil on Chart 1, and say **The pen is long. The pencil is short** and translate the new words as you go. For the word "long" make a sweeping action with your hand away from your body. For the word "short" bring your hand to within a few inches of your body. Next, introduce the concept of contractions by miming the idea clearly while you say **The pen is long – contraction? The <u>pen's</u> long. The pencil is short – contraction? The <u>pencil's</u> short**. Next, point to the long pen and ask **Is the pen long?** Then point to the short pencil and ask **Is the pencil short?** Always use this kind of question after you have just introduced a new word, as it only requires an easy positive answer. Do not, however, use it afterwards in lessons of revision when the questions must be of a type that requires a negative answer in order to force the students to speak as much as possible, and also to recall the opposite of the word used in the question.

Point to the long pen, and ask

Is the pen short?

No, the pen isn't short; it's long

Point to the short pencil, and ask

Is the pencil long?

No, the pencil isn't long; it's short

Is the room short?

No, the room isn't short; it's long

For the last question, you could use the name of a street in the student's home town instead of the word "room".

large   small

Point to your table, and then to the box on Chart 1, and say **The table's large. The box's small** – everything, of course, being relative. For the word "large", become expansive and spread your arms forward and round sideways. For the word "small" put your hands tightly together into a little ball. Then ask **Is the table large? Is the box small?** Next, ask

Is the table small?

No, the table isn't small; it's large

Is the box large?

No, the box isn't large; it's small

city   **town**   **village**

Explain to the students that **London is a city**. **Windsor is a town**. **Grantchester is a village**. Naturally, choose cities, towns and villages that the students are familiar with in their own part of the world. Then ask **Is (London) a city? Is (Windsor) a town? Is (Grantchester) a village?** Finally, ask the questions

Is (London) a village?   No, (London) isn't a village; it's a city

Is (Windsor) a city?   No, (Windsor) isn't a city; it's a town

Is (Grantchester) a town?   No, (Grantchester) isn't a town;
                    it's a village

or

Is the table long or short?   The table's ...

Is a city large or small?   A city's large

 See Chart 1

man   woman   boy   girl

Point to the figures on the Chart and say **This is a man. This is a woman. This is a boy. This is a girl**. As you say "man, woman" etc. just translate the one new word and not the whole sentence. Then, pointing again, just say **man; woman; boy; girl**. This is to bring out the important word in the sentence and to prevent it from being confused with the other words "This is a". It is always important to isolate a new word in order to make it easier to absorb. Next, point to the figures again and ask **Is this a man? Is this a woman? Is this a boy? Is this a girl?** Finally, pointing to each figure again in turn, ask

What's this?   It's a man. It's a woman. It's a boy. It's a girl.

Then point to the man, and ask

Is this a girl?   No, it isn't a girl; it's a man

Point to the woman, and ask

Is this a man?   No, it isn't a man; it's a woman

Point to the boy, and ask

Is this a woman?   No, it isn't a woman; it's a boy

Point to the girl, and ask

Is this a boy?   No, it isn't a boy; it's a girl

one	**two**	**three**	**four**	**five**
1	2	3	4	5

Hold up your fingers one at a time, and, as you do so, count the numbers from one to five. Repeat this quickly two or three times, then go quickly round the class getting each student in turn to say a number as you hold up your fingers.

on	**under**	**in**

Put a pen, first on a book, then under the book, then in the book while saying **The pen's on the book. The pen's under the book. The pen's in the book**. Then ask **Is the pen on the book? Is the pen under the book? Is the pen in the book?** Next, put the pen under the book, and ask

Is the pen in the book?   No, the pen isn't in the book;
                                                                        it's under the book

Put the pen on the book, and ask

Is the pen under the book?   No, the pen isn't under the book;
                                                                          it's on the book

See Chart 1

Mr   Mrs   Jack   Anna

Point to the figures on Chart 1 and say **This is Mr Brown. This is Mrs Brown. This is Jack Brown. This is Anna Brown**. Then ask **Is this Mr Brown? Is this Mrs Brown? Is this Jack Brown? Is this Anna Brown?** Explain, if necessary, that the word "Brown" is just a surname used as an example.

Point to Mr Brown, and ask

Is this Anna Brown?   No, it isn't Anna Brown; it's Mr Brown

Point to Mrs Brown, and ask

Is this Mr Brown?   No, it isn't Mr Brown; it's Mrs Brown

Point to Jack Brown, and ask

Is this Mrs Brown?   No, it isn't Mrs Brown; it's Jack Brown

Point to Anna Brown, and ask

Is this Jack Brown?   No, it isn't Jack Brown; it's Anna Brown

See Chart 1

black   white   green   brown

what colour?

Point to the black, white, green and brown pencils on Chart 1, and say **This pencil's black. This pencil's white. This pencil's green. This pencil's brown**. Repeat this once or twice. Then ask **What colour's this pencil?** and translate. Then, pointing to each pencil in turn, ask

What colour's this pencil?   This pencil's black, white etc.

six	seven	eight	nine	ten
6	7	8	9	10

Repeat the same procedure as with the numbers from one to five.

where

Put the pen on the book, under the table, in the book etc., and ask

Where's the pen?   The pen's on the book

Where's the book?   The book's on the table

Where's the pen?   The pen's under the table

Where's the picture?   The picture's on the wall

Where's the light?   The light's on the ceiling

LESSON 2

 *See Chart 1*

I am	**I'm**
you are	**you're**
he is	**he's**
she is	**she's**
it is	**it's**

This part can be complicated and may need constant translation and repetition. You may also find it easier to introduce "I'm" and "you're" separately from "he's" and "she's". Always use the contracted forms in speaking, and when the students come to read, explain that we use the contracted forms in speaking and the long forms in writing.

Point to yourself, the student, then Mr and Mrs Brown, and say and translate two or three times **I'm ...; You're ...; He's Mr Brown; She's Mrs Brown**. Next, ask and translate **Am I? Are you? Is he? Is she?** Then, finally ask

Am I ...?	Yes, you're ...
Are you ...?	Yes, I'm ...
Is he Mr Brown?	Yes, he's Mr Brown
Is she Mrs Brown?	Yes, she's Mrs Brown

I am not	**I'm not**
you are not	**you aren't**
he is not	**he isn't**
she is not	**she isn't**
it is not	**it isn't**

Do not teach the alternatives "you're not" etc. It will confuse the students. Never teach alternatives at the beginning. It is difficult enough for the student to learn one thing at a time, without the teacher complicating matters by giving him alternatives. The alternatives can be learnt later, naturally and easily.

Am I Mrs Brown?   No, you aren't Mrs Brown; you're …

Point to the student, and ask

Are you Mr Brown?   No, I'm not Mr Brown; I'm …

Point to Mr Brown, and ask

Is he Mr Smith?   No, he isn't Mr Smith; he's Mr Brown

Point to Mrs Brown, and ask

Is she Mr Brown?   No, she isn't Mr Brown; she's Mrs Brown

in front of   **behind**   **me**   **you**

Put your chair in front of you, then behind you, and say **The chair's in front of me. The chair's behind me.** Accompany this with appropriate hand actions to indicate "in front of", "behind", and "me". Actions are very important at this stage of learning. Next, point to the student, and say **The table's in front of you. The wall's behind you**. Then ask **Is the chair in front of me? Is the chair behind me? Is the table in front of you? Is the wall behind you?** Finally ask

Where's the table?   The table's in front of me

When asking the above question, hit the table with your finger, and make an action to indicate that the table is in front of the student, so that they know what to reply; otherwise they might look puzzled, or say "The table is on the floor". This kind of thing applies to any question that may appear ambiguous. The teacher must make it clear what they want the student to reply, and so not waste time while the student puzzles over what they are supposed to say. Next, ask

Is the wall in front of you?

No, the wall isn't in front of me; it's behind me

Shake your head when asking this question, and point to the wall behind the student, so that they know they must answer negatively, because a wall is certain to be in front of them, though not the one you intend.

Is the table behind me?

No, the table isn't behind you; it's in front of you

 *See Chart 1*

him   her   house

Point to yourself, the student, Mr and Mrs Brown, and the house, and say **The wall's behind me. The wall's behind you. The house's behind him. The house's behind her**. Then repeat, and translate once or twice **me; you; him; her**. Accompany all this with actions. For example, for the sentence "The wall's behind me", point to the wall, move your hand as if you were throwing something over your shoulder, and then thump your chest. The students will understand the word "house" from the picture. Then ask **Is the house behind him? Is the house behind her?**

Point to the house and Mr Brown, and make a movement which means behind him (do the same with Mrs Brown), and ask

Where's the house?

The house is behind him

Where's the house?

The house is behind her

The student might answer "Mr Brown" instead of "him". If so, say the word "him" in a questioning tone in the student's own language; meaning that you want them to give you the English translation. This way of eliciting an answer from a student is always very useful. Next, hold up Chart 1 in front of you and, pointing in turn to Mrs Brown and then Mr Brown, ask

Are you behind her?

No, I'm not behind her; I'm in front of her

Am I in front of him?

No, you aren't in front of him; you're behind him

standing   sitting

While performing the appropriate actions, say **I'm standing on the floor. I'm sitting on the chair**. Then ask **Am I standing on the floor? Am I sitting on the chair?** Then ask

Are you standing on the floor?

No, I'm not standing on the floor; I'm sitting on the chair

Am I sitting on the chair?

No, you aren't sitting on the chair; you're standing on the floor

Are you standing in front of me?

No, I'm not standing in front of you; I'm sitting in front of you

Do not forget to point clearly at the student every time you say "you", and at yourself when you say "I" or "me". Always accompany everything you say with actions. They make it easier for students to understand and keep their attention on you.

taking from   putting on

Take the book from the table, then put it on the table, saying **I'm taking the book from the table. I'm putting the book on the table**. Then ask **Am I taking the book from the table? Am I putting the book on the table?**

Take the book from the table, and ask

Am I putting the book on the floor?

No, you aren't putting the book on the floor; you're taking the book from the table

Am I taking the pen from the table?

No, you aren't taking the pen from the table; you're putting the book on the table

opening   closing

Open and close the book, and say **I'm opening the book. I'm closing the book**. Then ask **Am I opening the book? Am I closing the book?** Finally

Open the book, and ask

Am I closing the door?

No, you aren't closing the door; you're opening the book

Close the book, and ask

Am I opening the window?

No, you aren't opening the window; you're closing the book

doing   what am I doing?

The question "What am I doing?" may need constant translation, even in future revisions. Pick up a book, open it, close it, and put it on the table while asking

What am I doing?
You're taking the book from the table

What am I doing?
You're opening the book

What am I doing?
You're closing the book

What am I doing?
You're putting the book on the table

 See Chart 1

which

This word may need frequent translation, as some students may find difficulty in remembering words beginning with a "w". They especially tend to confuse words like "where", "which", "what", "when", "who", "why" etc. Point simultaneously to the black and white pencils on the Chart (doing the same with the green and brown pencils), and ask

Which pencil's black?	This pencil's black

As the students have to point at the pencil while answering, take the Chart near to them.

Which pencil's white?	This pencil's white
Which pencil's green?	This pencil's green
Which pencil's brown?	This pencil's brown

open   **closed**

Hold up an open book and a closed book, and ask

Which book's open?	This book's open
Which book's closed?	This book's closed

"Open" and "closed" should be understood without difficulty from the verbs already learnt. With any word or phrase that students find difficulty in understanding or remembering, or that you think they have forgotten, keep asking in their own language "What does the word … mean?" When you come to the word "mean" in the book, you can then ask them the question in English.

LESSON 3

See Chart 1

this	that	chart

For these questions, you could stick a white pencil on the wall at the back of the classroom. Then, pointing to the black pencil on the Chart, say **This pencil's black** and, pointing to the white pencil on the wall, say **That pencil's white**. Next, take the Chart to the student, and ask

What colour's this pencil?
This pencil's black

Addressing the same student, point to the white pencil on the wall, and ask

What colour's that pencil?
That pencil's white

Where's this pencil?
This pencil's on the Chart

Where's that pencil?
That pencil's on the wall

eleven	twelve	thirteen	fourteen	fifteen
11	12	13	14	15

Adopt the same procedure as with the numbers from one to five, but first put up all ten digits, and say "ten", then get the students to count as you hold up your fingers individually.

plural	of	etc.

The plural of "book" is "books" – one book, two books; one pen, two pens etc. Words like "of", "say" and "etc." in explanations can be translated as you go along, though their meaning can often be guessed at by the students. Later, such words will be treated fully.

What's the plural of "book"?   The plural of "book" is "books"

What's the plural of "clock"?   The plural of "clock" is "clocks"

What's the plural of "wall"?   The plural of "wall" is "walls"

we are   we're

I'm sitting and you're sitting. We're sitting.

Are we sitting?   Yes, we're sitting

Where are we sitting?   We're sitting on the chairs

 See Chart 1

they are   they're

Point to Mr and Mrs Brown, and say **He's standing and she's standing. They're standing**. Then ask

Are they standing?   Yes, they're standing

Where are they standing?   They're standing in front of the house

With the above question, you will need to make it clear through actions that you want the student to answer "in front of the house", otherwise he might say "on the floor".

we are not   we aren't

Are we standing?   No, we aren't standing; we're sitting

Are we sitting on the floor?   No, we aren't sitting on the floor; we're sitting on the chairs

they are not   **they aren't**

Point to Mr and Mrs Brown, and ask

Are they sitting?   No, they aren't sitting; they're standing

Are they standing behind the house?   No, they aren't standing behind the house; they're standing in front of the house

red   **blue**   **yellow**   **grey**

 *See Chart 1*

Point to the pencils on the Chart and follow the same procedure as with the black, white, green and brown pencils by saying **This pencil's red etc**. Then ask

What colour's this pencil?   This pencil's red, blue etc.

these   **those**   **and**

For these questions, you could stick a brown pencil on the wall at the back of the classroom, as you did with the white pencil. Then, pointing to the black pencil on the Chart and to the white pencil on the wall, say **This pencil's black. That pencil's white**. (Repeat the words "this" and "that"). Next, point to the black and the green pencils on the Chart and the white and brown pencils on the wall, and say **These pencils are black and green. Those pencils are white and brown**. (Repeat the words **these** and **those**.)

What colour's this pencil?   This pencil's black

What colour's that pencil?   That pencil's white

What colour are these pencils?   These pencils are black and green

What colour are those pencils?

Those pencils are white and brown

Where are these pencils?

These pencils are on the Chart

Where are those pencils?

Those pencils are on the wall

What colour are these chairs?

These chairs are ...

What colour are those chairs?

Those chairs are ...

men   women   say

The plural of "man" is "men". We say one "man", and two "men". The plural of "woman" is "women". We say one "woman", and two "women".

What's the plural of "man"?

The plural of "man" is "men"

What's the plural of "woman"?

The plural of "woman" is "women"

sixteen   seventeen   eighteen   nineteen   twenty
16   17   18   19   20

Use the same procedure as with the numbers from 11 to 15.

 See Chart 1

clothes

Touch all your clothes, and say **These are clothes** (and translate). Then ask

What are these?

These are clothes

shoe	boot	sock	trousers	jacket

suit	shirt	tie	hat	bag

In order to go faster, especially in the revisions, instead of wasting time looking for the Chart, and so giving the students' attention the opportunity to wander, you can point to your own articles of clothing and to those of the students. You can mime "hat" and "coat" by pretending to put on a hat and coat. If you cannot find all the articles of clothing among the class, and if your miming is too slow and unsuccessful, then it will be easier to use the Chart; though, while you are looking for it, you can start with the clothes you and the students are wearing. A list of words like the above is always difficult for the students to learn. It is not important, therefore, if they cannot remember them first time; like all other words, they will be repeated several times. Take only three objects at a time, and ask

What's this?

It's a shoe, boot etc.

What are these?

These are trousers

 *See Chart 2*

alphabet	letter

Read out the alphabet once or twice at normal speed. Then, beginning at the letter A and going clockwise or systematically round the class, get each student to pronounce a letter.

What letter's this?

A, B, etc.

vowel	consonant

Point to the vowels and say **These are the five vowels: A, E, I, O, U**. Then ask

What are these?

These are the five vowels

What are the five vowels?

The five vowels are A, E, I ,O, U

The letters B, C, D etc. are consonants.

Is the letter B a vowel?

No, the letter B isn't a vowel;
it's a consonant

before	after

Explain that **The letter A's before the letter B; and the letter C's after the letter B**. At the same time make the appropriate hand actions, such as brushing your hand away from the letters in question. Repeat the words **before** and **after**. Then ask

Which letter's before E?

D's before E

Which letter's after I?

J's after I

Which letter's before Z?

Y's before Z

Which letter's after G?

H's after G

LESSON 4

between

The letter B's between the letter A and the letter C.

Which letter's between D and F?   E's between D and F

Which letter's between H and J?   I's between H and J

Which letter's between Q and S?   R's between Q and S

us

Explain that **The table's in front of me. The table's in front of you. The table's in front of us**. Next ask **Is the table in front of us?** Finally ask

Where's the table?   The table's in front of us

For the above question, point to the table, make an action meaning "in front of" and then keep pointing to yourself and the student, so that they know what to answer.

Are the walls in front of us?   No, the walls aren't in front of us; they're behind us

Is the table behind us?   No, the table isn't behind us; it's in front of us

 *See Chart 1*

them

Point to Mr and Mrs Brown, and say **The house's behind him. The house's behind her. The house's behind them**. Then ask **Is the house behind them?** For greater clarity you could point to yourself, the student etc. and say **"me, you, him, her, it, us, you, them"**. Finally ask

Where's the house?

The house's behind them

Immediately after asking the above question, point to the house, make a movement meaning "behind", and then point with two fingers at the same time to Mr and Mrs Brown, so that the student is in no doubt as to what he is to answer. Then, holding the Chart in front of you, ask

Are you behind them?

No, I'm not behind them;
I'm in front of them

Am I in front of them?

No, you aren't in front of them;
you're behind them

student   teacher

Look at a student and explain that **I'm the teacher. You're a student**. Then ask **Am I the teacher? Are you a student?** Finally ask

Am I a student?

No, you aren't a student; you're the teacher

Are you the teacher?

No, I'm not the teacher; I'm a student

 See Chart 3

thirty	**forty**	**fifty**	**sixty**	**seventy**	**eighty**
30	40	50	60	70	80

ninety	**hundred**	**thousand**	**million**	**number**
90	100	1,000	1,000,000	

Count the numbers from 30, down the column, to 1,000,000 on the Chart once or twice, then go round the class asking

What number's this?

30, 40 etc.

Next, count the numbers from 30 to 90, then from 13 to 19, lengthening the "teen" sound as you do so. Then read out 30–13; 40–14 etc. to show the difference in pronunciation. Next make the students run down both columns including 100, 1,000 and 1,000,000, and then get them in turn to count across "30–13" etc. Also get the students to pronounce the other numbers on the Chart, "313" etc., stressing the "and" before the last number pronounced.

What numbers are these?

30–13; 40–14 etc.

What number's this?

313   1,815   1,950,630

plus   equals   2 + 2 = 4

Point to the Chart and explain that **2 + 2 = 4**. Then ask

What's this?

It's 2 + 2 = 4

how much

How much is 13 plus 5?

13 plus 5 equals 18

for children

How much is   18 + 40   5 + 10
                     60 + 19   6 + 3
                     16 + 30   20 + 15
                     90 + 15   10 + 30

As the answers are being given, point to the numbers on the Chart, just in case some of the students do not understand. After three or four revisions, children might be able to do the adult sums.

Below is the instruction for the teacher to ask the students to read Lesson 1. Until now, if it has been possible, the students should not have opened their books. They should have learnt everything by ear in order to acquire the teacher's pronunciation. If they see the words before they have mastered the sounds, they are more likely to pronounce them as they are written, as visual memory is usually stronger than aural memory.

The reading of past lessons also acts as a revision of past work. The questions and answers should be divided equally among the students, so that everybody has the same opportunity to read. The teacher can get the students to read in a set order, so that all he has to say is "Next" when a student stops reading. But, if they are inattentive and it is a large class, it is probably better for the teacher to call students by name at random, so that no one knows when his turn is coming. This means each student must pay constant attention and not lose his place in the book.

 *Students read Lesson 1 on page 1*

there is   there's

There's a pen on the book. There's a picture on the wall. There's a table in this room.
"There's" and "there are" may need frequent translation. Next, take a book and a pen near to a student and ask

Is there a pen on this book?	Yes, there's a pen on this book
Is there a light on the ceiling?	Yes, there's a light on the ceiling
Is there a bag in this room?	Yes, there's a bag in this room

there are   now

There's one pen on the book. There are two pens on the book now. The word "now" can be translated as you go along. Make sure the students put "there's" and "there are" at the beginning of the sentence and not anywhere else.

Is there a pen on the book?	Yes, there's a pen on the book
Are there two pens on the book now?	Yes, there are two pens on the book now

Are there (12) chairs in this room?

Yes, there are (12) chairs in this room

Are there (2) pictures on these walls?

Yes, there are (2) pictures on these walls

there is not   there isn't

Is there a pen on the book?

No, there isn't a pen on the book

Is there a book on the floor?

No, there isn't a book on the floor

Is there a clock on the table?

No, there isn't a clock on the table

there are not   there aren't

Are there three clocks on that wall?

No, there aren't three clocks on that wall; there's one clock on that wall

Are there a hundred pictures in this room?

No, there aren't a hundred pictures in this room; there are ... pictures in this room

Are there a thousand chairs in this room?

No, there aren't a thousand chairs in this room; there are ... chairs in this room

high   low   but

The wall's high, but the chair's low.

Is the chair high?

No, the chair isn't high; it's low

Is the wall low?

No, the wall isn't low; it's high

Is the table high?

No, the table isn't high; it's low

LESSON 5

| imperative | take! | put! | open! |

| close! | please |

Explain that **The imperative is "take!", "put!", "open!", "close!" etc**. Then, pointing to a book and making a taking action, but without touching the book, say to a student

Take the book, please.

Then ask a second student

What's he/she doing?   He's/She's taking the book

Make one student do all the following actions while the other students, in turn, answer.

Open the book, please.

What's he/she doing?   He's/She's opening the book

Close the book, please.

What's he/she doing?   He's/She's closing the book

Put the book on the table, please.

What's he/she doing?   He's/She's putting the book on the table

 *See Chart 1*

here   there

Point to the black pencil on the Chart in front of you and the white pencil on the wall, and say **The black pencil's here. The white pencil's there** (repeat the words **here** and **there**). Then ask **Is the black pencil here? Is the white pencil there?** Naturally, ask a student who is sitting near the black pencil for the word "here" and one who is far from the white pencil for the word "there". With the following questions, make it quite clear which answer you expect by pointing downwards emphatically in front of the student for "here" and at a distance for "there".

Where's the black pencil?	The black pencil's here in front of me
Where's the white pencil?	The white pencil's there on the wall
Are you sitting there?	No, I'm not sitting there; I'm sitting here
Is the white pencil here in front of you?	No, the white pencil isn't here in front of me; it's there on the Chart

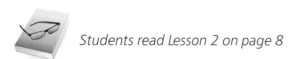 *Students read Lesson 2 on page 8*

capital   England   Russia   Greece   China

London   Moscow   Athens   Beijing

Explain that **London's the capital of England. Moscow's the capital of Russia. Athens's the capital of Greece. Beijing's the capital of China**. For the following questions, insist on the student answering "London's the capital of England" etc., and not "The capital of England is London".

What's the capital of England?	London's the capital of England
What's the capital of Russia?	Moscow's the capital of Russia

What's the capital of Greece?	Athens's the capital of Greece
What's the capital of China?	Beijing's the capital of China

reading   writing

Explain with appropriate actions that **I'm reading the book. Now, I'm writing in the book**. Then ask **Am I reading the book? Am I writing in the book?** Finally, ask

What am I doing?	You're reading the book
What am I doing?	You're writing in the book
Am I writing in the book?	No, you aren't writing in the book; you're reading the book
Am I reading the book?	No, you aren't reading the book; you're writing in the book

 *See Chart 1*

coat   tights   dress   skirt   scarf

blouse   pullover   pocket   handkerchief

What's this?	It's a coat, dress etc.
What are these?	These are tights

how many?

Translate as you ask the following first question. Make sure the student answers with "there's" in the fourth question, and not with "there are".

How many pictures are there on these walls?	There are ... pictures on these walls
How many clocks are there in this room?	There's one clock in this room
How many chairs are there in this room?	There are ... chairs in this room
How many teachers are there in this room?	There's one teacher in this room

going to

Walk towards the window, then the door, then the wall, while saying **I'm going to the window. I'm going to the door. I'm going to the wall**. When saying the word "to", point forcefully to the object you are approaching. Next, ask **Am I going to the window? Am I going to the door? Am I going to the wall?**

What am I doing?	You're going to the door
What am I doing?	You're going to the window
Where am I going?	You're going to the wall
Am I going to the door?	No, you aren't going to the door; you're going to the window

LESSON 6

Europe   Asia   Italy   France   India

Explain that **Italy's in Europe. France's in Europe. China's in Asia. India's in Asia etc**. Then ask

Is Greece in Asia?

No, Greece isn't in Asia; it's in Europe

Is India in Europe?

No, India isn't in Europe; it's in Asia

Are France and Italy in Asia?

No, France and Italy aren't in Asia; they're in Europe

 See Chart 2

first	**second**	**third**	**fourth**
1st	2nd	3rd	4th

fifth	**sixth**	**twelfth**	**twentieth**
5th	6th	12th	20th

cardinal   ordinal

Point to the letters A, B and C and say **A's the first letter of the alphabet, B's the second letter of the alphabet, and C's the third letter of the alphabet**. Hold up your fingers and repeat **first; second; third**. Then ask **Which's the first letter of the alphabet? Which's the second letter of the alphabet? Which's the third letter of the alphabet?** Stress the pronunciation of the word "the" before the word "alphabet", but do not comment on it.

Point out that **We say first, second and third but, after that, all the ordinal numbers finish in "th"**. Point out also that **The cardinal numbers are "one, two, three etc.", and the ordinal numbers are "first, second, third etc."**

What are the cardinal numbers?	The cardinal numbers are 1, 2, 3, etc.
What are the ordinal numbers?	The ordinal numbers are 1st, 2nd, 3rd, etc.

Finally, beginning with the letter A, go systematically round the class asking each student to say an ordinal number as you point to each letter of the alphabet. Point out the pronunciation of "twentieth", and stress the definite article before each number.

Then ask

Which is the first letter of the alphabet?	A's the first letter of the alphabet
Which is the third letter of the alphabet?	C's the third letter of the alphabet
Which is the fifth letter of the alphabet?	E's the fifth letter of the alphabet
Which is the twelfth letter of the alphabet?	L's the twelfth letter of the alphabet
Which is the thirteenth letter of the alphabet?	M's the thirteenth letter of the alphabet
Which is the twentieth letter of the alphabet?	T's the twentieth letter of the alphabet
Which is the twenty-first letter?	U's the twenty-first letter
Which is the twenty-third letter?	W's the twenty-third letter
Which is the twenty-fifth letter?	Y's the twenty-fifth letter

last

The word "last" is introduced naturally at the end of the above list, and should be easily understood if you give a quick horizontal cut of your hand.

Which's the last letter of the alphabet?

Z's the last letter
of the alphabet

Is A the last letter of the alphabet?

No, A isn't the last
letter of the alphabet; it's
the first letter of the alphabet

give

Ask the student to take the book. Then, holding out your hand, ask the student to give you the book. Do not confuse the students by giving them the alternative form "Give the book to me". This form is possibly less used, and one thing at a time is enough.

Take the book, please.

Give me the book, please.

Then, to a second student, ask

What's he/she doing?

He's/She's giving you the book

Take the book, please.

Give him/her the book, please.

Then, to a third student, ask

What's he/she doing?

He's/She's giving him/her the book

 Students read Lesson 3 on page 14

French	**German**	**Italian**	**English**

Are you (French) or (German)?

No, I'm not (French) or (German); I'm ...

Am I (Italian) or (French)?

No, you aren't (Italian) or (French); you're (English)

Are the students (German) or (English)?

The students are ...

For the above questions, change the words according to the nationality of the students.

my   your

Point to the relevant books, and explain that **This is my book, and that is your book**. Then ask **Is this my book? Is that your book?** Next, indicate your book and say

Is this your book?

No, it isn't my book; it's your book

Then point to something the student is wearing, and ask

Is that my dress?

No, it isn't your dress; it's my dress

 *See Chart 1*

his   her

Point to Mr and Mrs Brown, and say **These are his shoes, and these are her shoes**. Then ask **Are these his shoes? Are these her shoes? For a man we say "his"; for a woman we say "her"**.

Point to Mrs Brown's boots, then to Mr Brown, and ask

Are these his boots?

No, they aren't his boots; they're her boots

Point to Mr Brown's shoes, then to Mrs Brown, and ask

Are these her shoes?

No, they aren't her shoes; they're his shoes

Point to Mrs Brown's bag, then to Mr Brown, and ask

Is this his bag?

No, it isn't his bag; it's her bag

Point to Mr Brown's suit, then to Mrs Brown, and ask

Is this her suit?

No, it isn't her suit; it's his suit

What colour's his suit?

His suit's black

our   your   their

Explain that **This is my book. That is your book. These are our books**. Then, pointing to Mr and Mrs Brown, explain that **These are his shoes. These are her shoes. These are** (pointing to them both together) **their shoes**.

Point to Mr and Mrs Brown's shoes, then at the student and yourself, and ask

Are these our shoes?

No, they aren't our shoes; they're their shoes

Point out here by heavy stressing that the words "they're" and "their" have a similar or even identical pronunciation.

What colour are their shoes?

Their shoes are black

Point to the student's book and your book, then at Mr and Mrs Brown, and ask

Are these their books?

No, these aren't their books; they're our books

Where are our books?

Our books are on the table(s)

From now on the demonstration questions will not be included. They are still to be asked, of course, and can easily be deduced from the demonstration sentences. For example **I am going to the window** is the demonstration sentence from which we ask **Am I going to the window?** as the demonstration question. Such a question is not asked in the revision. The type which takes its place is something like **What am I doing?** which forces the student to recall the words "going to" in their answer.

all

Explain that **All the walls in this room are white. All the books in this room are English books. All the students are sitting**. The word "all" has two positions in a sentence, i.e. "All the students are sitting" or "The students are all sitting". For the sake of simplicity, just teach the former position.

Are all the walls in this room white (or green or blue etc.)?

Yes, all the walls in this room are white

Are all the books in this room English books?

Yes, all the books in this room are English books

Are all the students sitting?

Yes, all the students are sitting

LESSON 7

person   people

Explain that **I'm a person; you're a person; Mr Brown's a person; Mrs Brown's a person etc. The plural of "person" is "people". We say "one person", but "two people**". Then ask

What's the plural of "person"?

The plural of "person" is "people"

How many people are there in this room?

There are … people in this room

How many people are there in this town?

There are … people in this town

If the student does not know the number of people there are in the place where he lives, tell him in his own language and get him to translate.

coming from

Go to the window and return, while saying **I'm going to the window. I'm coming from the window**. As you say the word "from" wave your hand as if you were pulling something or beckoning a car to overtake.

Come from the door, and ask

What am I doing?

You're coming from the door

Go to the window, and ask

Am I coming from the window?

No, you aren't coming from the window; you're going to the window

Come from the window, and ask

Am I going to the window?

No, you aren't going to the
window; you're coming from the window

touch

Explain with actions that **I'm touching the wall. I'm touching the book etc**. Touch these objects just with your fingertips to save misunderstanding.

What am I doing?

You're touching the wall

What am I doing?

You're touching the picture

Touch your tie (or dress, shoe etc.), please.

What's he/she doing?

He's/She's touching his/her ...

 See Chart 2

sentence

Point to the sentence "Verbs are words we use for actions" on Chart 2, translate it, and then say **This is a sentence.**

What's this?

It's a sentence

word   verb   use   for   action

Point to the sentence again and say **This is a word. This is the word "verbs". This is a word. This is the word "use". There are seven words in this sentence**. Do not worry about all the new words in the sentence. "Word" is the important word to be learnt. The other words are included just to help your explanation later of the present simple tense. They are not meant to be taught at this stage. Then ask

What's this?

It's a word

How many words are there in this sentence?

There are seven words in this sentence

Which's the first word of this sentence?

"Verbs" is the first word of this sentence

Which's the third word of this sentence?

"Words" is the third word of this sentence

Which's the fifth word of this sentence?

"Use" is the fifth word of this sentence

Which's the sixth word?

"For" is the sixth word of this sentence

Which's the last word?

"Actions" is the last word of this sentence

question mark	?	full stop	.
comma	,	colon	:
semi-colon	;		

Point to the Chart, and ask

What's this?

It's a question mark

What's this?

It's a full stop

What's this?

It's a comma

What's this?

It's a colon

What's this?

It's a semi-colon

 Students read Lesson 4 on page 20

umbrella

Point to the word "umbrella" on Chart 2, and say **This is the word "umbrella"**, then ask

What word's this?

It's the word "umbrella"

Is there an umbrella on the table?

No, there isn't an umbrella on the table

pronounce

Say the word **book** and then say **I'm pronouncing the word "book".** Say the word **umbrella** and say **I'm pronouncing the word "umbrella"**. Then ask **What am I doing?** Next, read the question and the answer on Chart 2 **(What colour is the book? The book is blue)** so the students hear the correct pronunciation of the words before being asked to pronounce them.

Point to the word "What" on the Chart, and say

Pronounce this word, please.

What

Then ask another student

What's he/she doing?

He's/She's pronouncing the word "what"

Pronounce this word, please.

Colour

Then ask another student

What's he/she doing?

He's/She's pronouncing the word "colour"

a   an   the /ðə/   the /ði:/

Point to the Chart, and explain that **We say a book, but an umbrella. The book, but the umbrella. Before a consonant we say "a" – a book. Before a vowel we say "an" – an umbrella. Before a consonant we say "the" – the book. Before a vowel we say "the" – the umbrella**. Then get a different student, in turn, to pronounce each of the words.

Pronounce these words, please.

a book – **an** umbrella;
the book – **the** umbrella

body

Thump your chest and a few parts of your body, and say, and translate, **This is the body**.

What's this?   This is the body

Point to a female, or to Mrs Brown, and your own body, and ask

Is this her body?   No, it isn't her body; it's your body

part	foot	feet

Explain that **This part of the body is the foot. The plural of "foot" is "feet"**.

What part of the body is this?   This part of the body is the foot

What's the plural of "foot"?   The plural of "foot" is "feet"

leg	back	arm	wrist
hand	finger	thumb	

Point to the various parts of your body, taking three parts at a time, and ask (without commenting on "the" and "an")

What's this?   It's a leg, <u>the</u> back, <u>an</u> arm, a wrist etc.

right	**wrong**

Explain that **2 + 2 = 4 is right, but 2 + 2 = 5 is wrong**.

2 + 2 = 7: is that right?

No, it isn't right; it's wrong

The wall's high: is that wrong?

No, it isn't wrong; it's right

Is it right you're Mr Brown?

No, it isn't right I'm Mr Brown;
it's wrong. I'm ...

right **wrong**

LESSON 8

See Chart 2

question   answer

Point to the question and answer on Chart 2 (What colour is the book? The book is blue), and say **This is a question; this is an answer**.

What's this?

It's a question

What's this?

It's an answer

Is this an answer?

No, it isn't an answer; it's a question

meaning

Point to the words on Chart 2, and explain that **The meaning of the word "use" in ... is "...". The meaning of the word "for" in ... is "...". The meaning of the word "action" in ... is "..."**. Fill in the empty spaces with the words in the student's own language. For example, the meaning of the word "use" in Italian is "usare".

What's the meaning of the word "use" in ...?

The meaning of the word "use" in ... is "..."

What's the meaning of the word "table" in ...?

The meaning of the word "table" in ... is "..."

What's the meaning of the word "for" in ...?

The meaning of the word "for" in ... is "..."

What's the meaning of the word "chair" in ...?

The meaning of the word "chair" in ... is "..."

What's the meaning of the word "action" in ...?

The meaning of the word "action" in ... is "..."

The words "mean" and "meaning" are very useful words to be used a lot in the future in order to ask the student "What does the word ... mean?" whenever you think he has forgotten the meaning of a word.

name

Explain that **My name's ...; your name's ...; his name's Mr Brown**. Notice that, in the questions below, you are revising the possessive adjectives "my", "your" etc., so you need to stress them. Then ask

What's my name?   Your name's ...

What's your name?   My name's ...

 See Chart 1

Point to Mr and Mrs Brown (or to two other students), and ask

What's his name?   His name's Mr Brown

What's her name?   Her name's Mrs Brown

| head | face | chin | mouth |

| nose | eye | ear | hair | tongue |

Explain that **This is the head. This is the face etc.** (taking three parts of the head at a time), then ask

What's this?   It's the head etc.

remaining

Spread the fingers of one hand wide giving a pressing down movement with the hand at the same time, and say "remaining". You may need to translate to make sure that the students do not think that "remaining" is just another word for "sitting".

Go to the window and ask

What am I doing?	You're going to the window
What am I doing?	You're coming from the window
Are you going to the window?	No, I'm not going to the window; I'm remaining on the chair

Go to the window again, and ask

Am I remaining on the chair?	No, you aren't remaining on the chair; you're going to the window

country   Spain

Explain that **England's a country. Spain's a country. France's a country**. Then ask

What's the name of your country?	... is the name of my country

What's the name of the country between England and Spain?

France's the name of the country between England and Spain

translate   into

First say **The book is on the table**. Then translate it into the students' own language. Then say **I'm translating a sentence from English into ...** . A literal translation is always preferable, providing it makes sense to the students.

 *See Chart 2*

Point to the sentence on Chart 2, and say

"Verbs are words we use for actions".

Then translate the sentence into the students' own language, and ask

What am I doing?	You're translating a sentence from English into ...

Translate this sentence, please: "I am a student".

What's he/she doing?	He's/She's translating a sentence from English into ...

Translate this sentence, please: "The wall's high".

What's he/she doing?	He's/She's translating a sentence from English into ...

Translate this sentence, please: "There are ten chairs in this room".

What's he/she doing?	He's/She's translating a sentence from English into ...

 Students read Lesson 5 on page 25

who

This word will probably need constant translation. Point to yourself, the student, the Brown family in Chart 1, or other students in the class, and ask

Who am I?	You're Mr Smith
Who are you?	I'm Mr Rossi
Who's he?	He's Jack Brown

Who's she?	She's Anna Brown
Who are they?	They're Mr and Mrs Brown

thing

Pick up different objects, and say **This is a thing. This is a thing etc**. Then ask

How many things are there on this book?	There are three things on that book
What's the name of this thing?	The name of that thing is a tie
What colour's this thing?	This thing's red

 *See Chart 1*

tall   short   Scandinavia

Explain that **Mr Brown's tall, but Anna Brown's short**. Then ask, while moving your hand high and low as you do so,

Is Mr Brown short?	No, Mr Brown isn't short; he's tall
Is Anna Brown tall?	No, Anna Brown isn't tall; she's short
Are the people of Scandinavia short?	No, the people of Scandinavia aren't short; they're tall

difference   whereas   that

Explain that **We use "tall" and "short" for people, whereas we use "high" and "low" for things**. Translate the word "whereas" as you proceed, and in the revision get the student to use it by giving him the word in his own language and making him translate. Do the same with the word "that" in the answer below. The word "tall" can, of course, be used for things, e.g. a tall building, but such exceptions would only confuse the students at this stage of their studies.

What's the difference between "tall" and "short" and "high" and "low"?

The difference between "tall" and "short" and "high" and "low" is that we use "tall" and "short" for people, whereas we use "high" and "low" for things

Dictations: A dictation is probably the most difficult part of learning English, so do not worry too much at the beginning if the students spell badly. English people themselves sometimes find difficulty in spelling. The dictations are arranged so as to put as many recently acquired words as possible into each sentence, in order not to waste time having the students write down words they have already mastered. For this reason, the dictations are composed of unconnected sentences.

Much later on, the dictations become more complex, and even relate part of a story. One of the functions of a dictation is to allow students time to concentrate on the slow, exact pronunciation of each word. This is something they have no time to do when answering questions orally. Without dictations, they may, for example, never notice the difference between the words "called" and "cold". Dictations can also revise points of grammar. For example, "We use the present simple for ..."

Do not read the dictation through before and after dictating; this wastes time. Dictate immediately at slightly slower than normal speaking speed, repeating each segment an average of three times, depending on the speed and ability of the students. If students are not sure of the spelling of a word, they should try to guess rather than leave a space, but they should not hold up the dictation. After dictating, the students open their books and correct their dictations themselves with a red pen, while the teacher walks around the room looking over their shoulders to see that they are correcting properly. Every now and then the teacher can collect up the dictations and mark them, in order to see what progress is being made, and to give marks if necessary. By marking the dictations immediately themselves, the students can see their mistakes while the pronunciation of the words is still ringing in their ears. In order to save time, the students should correct their dictations immediately after the lesson.

 *Dictation 1*

What's this?/ It's a pen./ Is this/ a pencil/ or a book?/ Is the/ long table/ black?/ No, it isn't;/ it's white./ The short box/ is green./ A city is large/ but a village/ is small./ Is Mr Brown/ a man?/ Yes, he is./ Is Anna Brown/ a boy or a girl?/ She's a girl./ One, two, three,/ four, five./ Is the clock/ on the table/ or under the chair?/ No,/ it's on the wall./ What colour/ is the ceiling?

LESSON 9

asking	answering

Pick up a pen and ask **What's this?** The student will answer **It's a pen**. Then you say **I'm asking you a question**. Pick up a book, and ask **What's this?** The student will answer **It's a book**. Then you ask **What am I doing?** and get a second student to answer **You're asking him/her a question**. With the word "answering" adopt the same procedure, i.e. pick up a pen, and ask **What's this?** and when the pupil answers **It's a pen** you say **I'm asking you a question, and you're answering my question**.

What's this?	It's a pen
What am I doing?	You're asking him/her a question
What's this?	It's a hand
Am I asking him/her a question?	Yes, you're asking him/her a question
What's this?	It's a head
What's he/she doing?	He's/She's answering your question
What's this?	It's a mouth
Is he/she answering my question?	Yes, he's/she's answering your question

Point to a student, and say

Ask him/her a question, please.

From this point on you can get the students to ask each other questions at the beginning of each lesson immediately you enter the classroom, while you are opening your book and finding your place etc. You can do the same again at the end of each lesson, while collecting up your books. In this way there is not a second's silence from the time you enter the room to the time you leave it. Thus there can be no time for boredom, distraction or indiscipline, and the lesson will be much easier to give. The moment, however, that you have arranged your books and found your place, stop the students asking each other questions and go straight into the question and answer work.

To have

I have	**I've**
you have	**you've**
he has	**he's**
she has	**she's**
it has	**it's**
we have	**we've**
you have	**you've**
they have	**they've**

The meaning of the verb "to have" is "...". We say "I have, you have, he has, she has, it has, we have, you have, they have". The contraction of "I have" is "I've"; "you have" – "you've"; "he has" – "he's" etc.

Stress "has" for the third person. For the answer to the second question below, go round the class getting each student to give a contraction. For example, you say "I have", then point to a student and he says "I've", and so on. As the students answer the questions with "have" and the parts of the body, point to the parts referred to, just in case the other students have not learnt them properly yet. For the questions that follow, you can use Chart 1, if necessary, or other students in the class.

What's the meaning of the verb "to have"?

The meaning of the verb "to have" is ...

What's the contraction of "I have, you have" etc.?

I've, you've etc.

got   with   generally

With the verb "have", we generally use the word "got" and we say "I've got", "you've got", "he's got" etc. We say "I have a pen" or "I have got a pen".

Have I got two eyes?	Yes, you've got two eyes
Have you got two ears?	Yes, I've got two ears
Has he got two legs?	Yes, he's got two legs
Has she got two hands?	Yes, she's got two hands

Point to yourself and the student, and ask

Have we got two heads?	Yes, we've got two heads
Have they got four arms?	Yes, they've got four arms

 Students read Lesson 6 on page 29

 See Chart 4

any? non-specific	yes, **some** no, **not any**
how many? specific	seven thirteen etc. **none**

specific	**non-specific**	**negative**

positive   **for example**   **important**

when

Show the students the Chart and explain that **The meaning of "any" and "some" is "...", but we use "any" in questions and negative sentences, and "some" in positive sentences. For example, we say "Are there any books on the table?" – "Yes, there are some books on the table", and we say "Are there any books on the floor?" – "No, there aren't any books on the floor".** When saying "yes" and "no" stress them, and at the same time nod or shake your head.

Also explain that **We use "any" in a non-specific question, when the number is not important. For example, "Are there any books on the table?" – "Yes, there are some books on the table", or "No, there aren't any books on the table". If the number is important, we use "How many" and there is a specific answer – "one", "two", "three" etc., or "none".**

The word "some" is sometimes used in questions such as "Would you like some tea?", but such usage would confuse students at this stage of their studies.

What is the meaning of the words "any" and "some"?

The meaning of the words "any" and "some" is ...

What's the difference between "any" and "some"?

The difference between
"any" and "some" is that we use
"any" in questions and negative sentences,
whereas we use "some" in positive sentences

any

Are there any books on this table?

Yes, there are some
books on this table

Are there any pictures on these walls?

Yes, there are some
pictures on these walls

Have you got any shoes on your feet?

Yes, I've got some shoes on my feet

not any

Are there any books on the floor?

No, there aren't any books on the floor

Are there any pictures on that chair?

No, there aren't any pictures on that chair

Are there any chairs on the table?

No, there aren't any chairs on the table

none   class   classroom

How many books are there on the table?

There are ... books on the table

How many books are there on the floor?

There are none

How many pictures are there on these walls?

There are ... pictures on these walls

How many pictures are there on that chair?

There are none

How many students are there in this classroom?

There are ... students in this classroom

How many students are there sitting on the floor?

There are none

 *Do Revision Exercise 1*

Revision Exercises

Throughout the earlier stages of the Callan books, you will intermittently come across instructions saying 'Do Revision Exercise …'. These instructions also appear in the Student's Books and refer to extra revision exercises located at the end of each stage. The exercises themselves are not included in the Teacher's Books since they are designed to be done and corrected by the student outside class time. They constitute a form of voluntary homework.

The reason that the references to these exercises appear in the Teacher's Books is so that you can remind your students when they are due to do the next exercise. This reminder alone should encourage the students to do them. However, the exercises are not to be done during the lessons as this would waste valuable lesson time. They should be done externally.

If, at the end of Stage 4, a student is still having difficulty with their written English, you can suggest that they repeat all the exercises at home. It is important, however, that such a measure is not resorted to until the student has reached the end of Stage 4. Up to that point, it is quite normal for an English learner's spelling to be rather poor. It will become more accurate with time, as they progress through the books and their spoken English improves.

At this point the teacher takes the students right back to the beginning and does a complete revision.

The first part of learning a language is always the most difficult and the most important, as the speed of all future work depends on how well it has been mastered. The students at this point may be progressing quite well, but a rapid revision right from the beginning will give them extra speed in understanding and answering that will carry them through future work at a much faster rate. The revision will also show if the students have forgotten any past work now that a certain period of time has elapsed. Furthermore, it will straighten out any confusion they may have suffered when first being introduced to the work.

If in the revision the students seem to have remembered everything, then the teacher need only ask one question for each word and only do the revision once. If on the other hand the students fail to remember a lot of the work, it may be necessary to ask all questions for each word, and do the revision twice. In learning a language, it is essential that the students get off to a good start, as, unlike many subjects, what is not done well today will have serious consequences tomorrow. If the students are already understanding and answering at top speed, that is, almost at the speed with which they would use their own language, then a revision will not be necessary.

Whenever doing a complete revision, the teacher should explain to the students what is happening; otherwise they might be puzzled as to why they are going over old ground again.

Examinations

At the end of each stage, an examination is provided to give both the students and the teachers the opportunity to assess progress made to the end of that stage. It also serves to show how much the students have absorbed, and how much revision is needed. The exam is to be given orally.

The stage exam section consists of:

(1)   a 'yes/no quiz' of 40 questions

(2)   a vocabulary test with 40 words from the previous stage

(3)   a dictation

The full examination is out of 100 marks: 40 marks each for the 'yes/no quiz' and the vocabulary test, and 20 marks for the dictation.

The Stage Exam

The teacher gives the exam orally. For the 'yes/no quiz', the students are told first that all they need to write is "Yes" or "No". The teacher asks each question twice, just like each question in the method. For the vocabulary test, the students should translate the given word into their language. This is only possible in monolingual classes.

Marking

(1) In the 'yes/no quiz', the students receive 1 mark for each correct answer, lose 1 mark for each incorrect answer, and receive nothing where an answer is not given. This is to discourage them from guessing. So, for example, if 35 answers are right, 3 are wrong and 2 are left blank, the score will be 32 out of 40.

(2) In the vocabulary test, the students receive 1 mark for each correct answer. No marks are deducted for an incorrect answer.

(3) The dictation has a total of 20 marks. For each mistake the students lose 1 mark, so 20 mistakes or more would result in a mark of 0. If the same word is spelt incorrectly twice, this counts as only one mistake.

The teachers can mark the papers themselves or get the students to exchange papers and mark each other's.

Yes / No Quiz

No 1) Is a city small?

No 2) Is London a village?

Yes 3) Is Mrs Brown a woman?

Yes 4) Is the table in front of you?

No 5) Is your pen under the table?

No 6) Is the teacher standing on the table?

Yes 7) Are the walls behind us?

No 8) Are you taking a pencil from the floor?

No 9) Am I opening the window?

No 10) Are you sitting on the floor?

Yes 11) Are there five vowels in the English alphabet?

Yes 12) Is the letter G before the letter H?

No 13) Is the letter B after the letter I?

Yes 14) Is the letter E between D and F?

No 15) Is the word "some" a negative word?

Yes 16) Two plus two equals ten. Is that wrong?

No 17) Are there a thousand students in this room?

Yes 18) Are all these letters vowels: A, O, U?

No 19) Is Athens the capital of Russia?

No 20) Am I writing in a book?

No 21) Is India in Europe?

Yes 22) Is E the fifth letter of the alphabet?

No 23) Are the people of Scandinavia short?

No 24) Is I the first letter of the alphabet?

Yes 25) Is Z the last letter of the alphabet?

No 26) Are you giving me a book?

Yes 27) Are you answering a question?

No 28) Is the plural of "foot" "foots"?

No 29) Have you got ten fingers?

Yes 30) Are you a person?

No 31) Are you coming from the window?

Yes 32) Have Mr and Mrs Brown got two chins?

No 33) Is it right you're the teacher?

No 34) Are you going to the door?

Yes 35) Is the ceiling high?

No 36) Are there any chairs on the table?

Yes 37) Am I asking you a question?

Yes 38) Have you got two shoes?

No 39) Has Mr Brown got two heads?

No 40) Is the wall low?

Vocabulary Test

1) this
2) tongue
3) clothes
4) those
5) where
6) that
7) which
8) doing
9) there
10) leg
11) name
12) hand
13) them
14) her
15) coat
16) how much
17) scarf
18) mouth
19) dress
20) how many

21) my
22) meaning
23) handkerchief
24) our
25) pronounce
26) body
27) wrist
28) back
29) wrong
30) touch
31) nose
32) arm
33) ear
34) hair
35) remaining
36) suit
37) country
38) translate
39) high
40) who

 *Dictation*

What's this?/ It's a light./ The table/ is not short;/ it is long./ A village is small,/ but a city is large./ Where is the light?/ It's on the ceiling./ Mr White/ is standing/ in front of the house,/ but Mrs Green/ is sitting behind it./ He is not Mr Low;/ he's Mr Black./ What am I doing?/ You are taking the book/ from the table,/ opening it,/ and putting it/ on the floor./ Who is she?/ She's Mrs Brown./ The plural of "man"/ is "men"./ Those women/ are closing the windows./ Which pencil is green?/ This pencil is.

STAGE 2

LESSON 10

See Chart 5

Present continuous

| home | speak | that |

Get the students to repeat the present continuous (as below) for all persons.

Present continuous (positive)

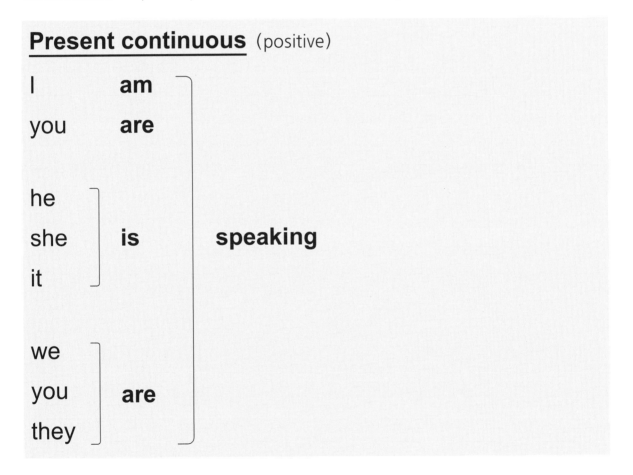

I	am	
you	are	
he		
she	is	speaking
it		
we		
you	are	
they		

Point to the chart and explain that **We use the present continuous for an action that we are doing now**. Perform appropriate actions while you are giving the following examples. **For example, I am going to the door; I am coming from the door; I am closing the book; I am opening the book**.

The Callan Method introduces contractions right from the beginning. In this lesson, however, it might be better to do the question and answer work initially without contractions. The main issue is whether the learner is able to distinguish the auxiliary "be" from the preceding subject pronoun. It is easy for a student to hear "He's speaking" and interpret it as "His speaking" or "He speaking". Also, some students (if they are real beginners) may still have problems with the forms of the subject pronouns themselves. As such, you should practise with <u>un</u>contracted forms in the answers if you feel your students are struggling in this area. Using full forms will help them distinguish word boundaries and identify the subject pronouns and the verb "be" as separate entities. That said, you should encourage the students to use contracted forms as soon as you feel they are competent in this area.

What am I doing?	You're opening the book
What am I doing?	You're closing the book
What am I doing?	You're going to the door
Are you speaking English?	Yes, I'm speaking English
Is he/she sitting on a chair?	Yes, he's/she's sitting on a chair

Get the students to repeat the present continuous (as below) for all persons.

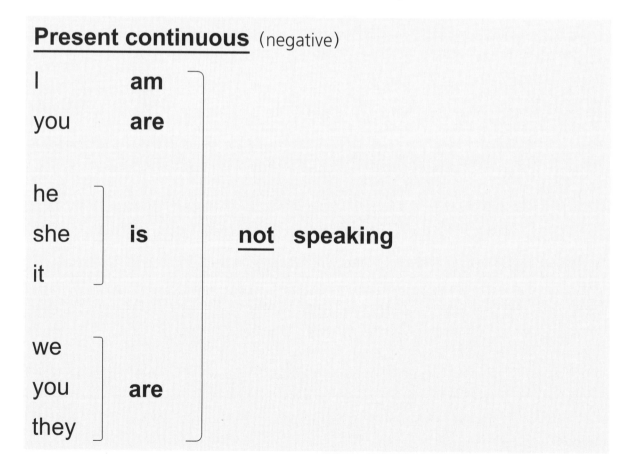

Present continuous (negative)

I	**am**		
you	**are**		
he			
she	**is**	**not**	**speaking**
it			
we			
you	**are**		
they			

For the negative, we say "not". For example, I am <u>not</u> speaking French; you are <u>not</u> standing on the table.

Am I writing in the book?

No, you aren't writing in the book; you're reading the book

Are you speaking ... (student's language)?

No, I'm not speaking ...; I'm speaking English

Is he standing on the floor?

No, he isn't standing on the floor; he's sitting on the chair

Is she speaking French?

No, she isn't speaking French; she's speaking English

Are we going home?

No, we aren't going home; we're remaining in the room

Point to Mr and Mrs Brown, and ask

Are they standing behind the house?

No, they aren't standing behind the house; they're standing in front of the house

Get the students to repeat the following.

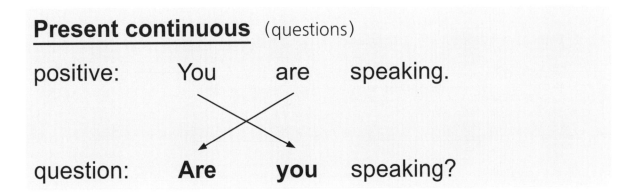

<u>Present continuous</u> (questions)

positive: You   are   speaking.

question: **Are   you   speaking?**

Point to the chart again and say **"You are speaking" is a positive sentence. For a question, we put "are" before "you" and we say "Are you speaking?"**

Are you sitting on a chair?

Yes, I'm sitting on a chair

What am I doing?

You're closing the book

Turn to one student, and say

Ask him/her a question with the present continuous.

What are you doing? Am I writing? etc.

 *See Chart 5*

Present simple	do	does
Japanese	**Chinese**	

Get the students to repeat the present simple (as below) for all persons.

Present simple (positive)

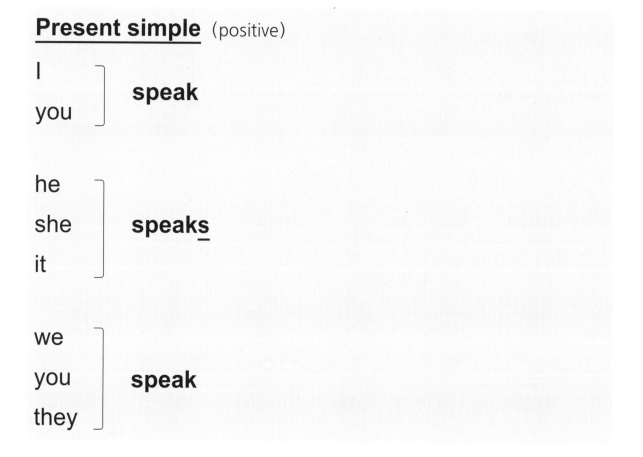

I
you ⎤ **speak**

he
she ⎤ **speaks**
it

we
you ⎤ **speak**
they

Point to the chart and explain that **We use the present continuous for an action we are doing now, whereas we use the present simple for an action we do generally. For example, now you are speaking English, but generally you speak ...** . Point to one student and say **He is not reading a book now, but generally he reads books**.

It is very important for students to understand this difference so, if necessary, explain the above in the students' own language if you can.

What's the difference between the present continuous and the present simple?

The difference between the present continuous and the present simple is that we use the present continuous for an action we are doing now, whereas we use the present simple for an action we do generally

With the present simple, we use the word "do". The word "do" hasn't got a meaning, but we use it in questions and negative sentences. For example, we say "Do you speak Japanese?" and "You do not speak Japanese".

Are you reading that book?

No, I'm not reading this book

Do you read that book?

Yes, I read this book

Are you writing?

No, I'm not writing

Do you write?

Yes, I write

Am I going to the door?

No, you aren't going to the door; you're remaining on the chair

Do I go to the door after the lesson?

Yes, you go to the door after the lesson

For "he", "she" and "it", we use the word "does". For example, we say "Does he speak Japanese?" and "He does not speak Japanese".

Is he going home?

No, he isn't going home; he's remaining in the room

Does he go home after the lesson?

Yes, he goes home after the lesson

57

Is she speaking?

Does she speak?

No, she isn't speaking

Yes, she speaks

do not   **don't**

does not   **doesn't**   **remain**

Get the students to repeat the present simple (as below) for all persons.

Present simple (negative)

I
you
do not speak

he
she
it
does not speak

we
you
they
do not speak

For the negative of the present simple, we use the words "do not" and we say "I do not speak Chinese". The contraction of "do not" is "don't" – "I don't speak Chinese". Obviously, if the students are speakers of Japanese, Chinese etc., change the languages appropriately throughout the following sections.

What's the negative of "I speak"?

The negative of "I speak" is "I don't speak"

Do you remain here after the lesson?

No, I don't remain here after the lesson; I go home

Point to Mr and Mrs Brown or some students, and ask

Do they speak Japanese?

No, they don't speak Japanese; they speak ...

Do I read books in Chinese?

No, you don't read books in Chinese; you read books in English

For "he", "she" and "it", we use the words "does not" for the negative, and we say "He does not speak Chinese". The contraction of "does not" is "doesn't" – "He doesn't speak Chinese".

What's the negative of "he speaks"?

The negative of "he speaks" is "he doesn't speak"

Point to a student, and ask

Does he/she speak Japanese?

No, he/she doesn't speak Japanese; he/she speaks ...

Does he/she remain here after the lesson?

No, he/she doesn't remain here after the lesson; he/she goes home after the lesson

Does he/she write in German?

No, he/she doesn't write in German; he/she writes in ...

Get the students to repeat the present simple (as below) for all persons.

Present simple (questions)

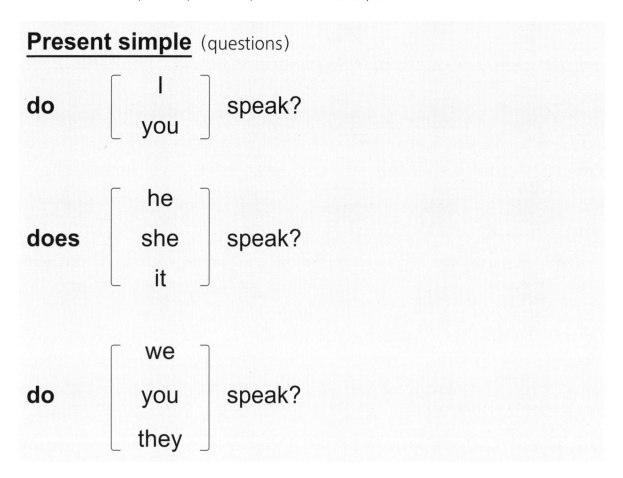

**For questions, we use the words "do" and "does", and we say "Do you speak Chinese?"
or "Does she write in German?"**

Point to a student, and say

Ask him/her a question with the word "do", please.

Do you speak English?
Do they read their books at home?

Ask him/her a question with the word "does", please.

Does he speak Chinese?
Does she read books in French?

 *Dictation 2*

You aren't Mrs Brown;/ you're Mr Green./ I'm Mrs Brown./ Six, seven, eight,/ nine, ten./ The women/ are standing/ under the light/ in front of/ the picture./ Where's the house?/ It's behind her./ What am I doing?/ You're taking the bag/ from me,/ closing it,/ and putting it/ on the floor./ Which door/ is open?/ That door is./ Eleven, twelve, thirteen,/ fourteen, fifteen.

If students correct their dictations in class, some will obviously finish before others. Those that do can ask each other questions.

LESSON 11

about   page

For the word "about", spread the fingers of one hand wide and move your hand like a ship rolling from side to side at sea. For the word "page", just lift up a page of your book.

About how many people are there in your country?

There are about ... people in my country

About how many things are there in this room?

There are about ... things in this room

About how many pages are there in this book?

There are about ... pages in that book

can

Translate the word "can" as you ask the question

Can you speak ...?

Yes, I can speak ...

Fill in the above space with the name of the student's own language.

Can you touch that book?

Yes, I can touch that (or this) book

Can you read and write?

Yes, I can read and write

like   dislike   cinema   television

"Don't like" is much more widely used in English than "dislike", but it is useful for students to know both.

Do you like your city (or town or village)?

Yes, I like my city ~ No, I don't like my city

Do you dislike the cinema?

No, I don't dislike the cinema;
I like the cinema

Do you like that picture?

Yes, I like that picture ~ No, I don't
like that picture; I dislike that picture

Do you dislike television?

No, I don't dislike television;
I like television

Referring to the previous student, ask

Does he/she dislike television?

No, he/she doesn't dislike
television; he/she likes television

right   left

This is my left hand and this is my right hand. Left. Right.

Which hand's this?

It's your left hand

Which hand's this?

It's your right hand

Put your right hand on that book, please.

What's he/she doing?

He/She is putting his/her
right hand on that book

Close your left eye, please.

What's he/she doing?

He/She is closing his/her left eye

moving   still   completely

Is my hand moving?

No, your hand isn't moving; it's still

Am I standing still?

No, you aren't standing still; you're moving

Are all the parts of your body still now?

No, not all the
parts of my body are still now;
my mouth and my tongue etc. are moving

63

Do you generally sit completely still in the lesson?

> No, I don't generally sit completely still in the lesson; I move

Does he/she generally sit completely still in the lesson?

> No, he/she doesn't generally sit completely still in the lesson; he/she moves

 Students read Lesson 7 on page 35

wearing   wear   glasses

Explain that **I'm wearing a tie. I'm wearing a shirt etc**. Do not let the student confuse "wear" with "where", which has the same pronunciation.

What clothes are you wearing?

> I'm wearing shoes, socks, a suit, etc.

Are you wearing glasses?

> Yes, I'm wearing glasses ~ No, I'm not wearing glasses

Are you wearing a hat?

> No, I'm not wearing a hat

Do you wear a hat?

> Yes, I wear a hat

Are you wearing a coat?

> No, I'm not wearing a coat

Do you wear a coat?

> Yes, I wear a coat

with

What am I doing?

> You're touching your nose with your finger

Do we speak with our mouths?

> Yes, we speak with our mouths

Do we read with our eyes?

> Yes, we read with our eyes

half

Two is half of four. Six is half of twelve.

How much is half of a hundred?

> Fifty is half of a hundred

How much is half of thirteen?

> Six and a half is half of thirteen

Are half of the people in this town men?

> Yes, half of the people in this town are men

tell

My name's Mr Smith. I'm telling you my name.

Tell me your name, please.

> My name's ...

What's he/she doing?

> He/She is telling you his/her name

Tell me the name of the capital of Russia, please.

> Moscow's the capital of Russia

What's he/she doing?

> He/She is telling you the name of the capital of Russia

LESSON 12

Russian	**Greek**
Are you (Russian) or (Greek)?	No, I'm not (Russian) or (Greek); I'm ...
Do you speak (Greek)?	No, I don't speak (Greek); I speak ...

prefer	**tea**	**coffee**

Which do you prefer: <u>the</u> cinema or television?	I prefer ... to ...
Which do you prefer: tea or coffee?	I prefer ... to ...
Which does he/she prefer: tea or coffee?	He/She prefers ... to ...
Do the English generally prefer coffee?	No, the English don't generally prefer coffee; they generally prefer tea

both

We use "both" for two people or things. Both my hands are on the table. Both of us are in the room. We aren't both sitting; you're sitting, but I'm standing.

Are both my hands on the table?	Yes, both your hands are on the table
Are both these books open?	Yes, both these books are open

We can say "both chairs" or "both of the chairs" but, with the words "us", "you" and "them", we say "both of us/you/them" and not "both us/you/them".

Which is it right to say: "both us" or "both of us"?

It's right to say "both of us"

Point to two students, and ask one of them

Are both of you sitting?

Yes, both of us are sitting

Point to two students, and ask a third student

Do both of them speak English?

Yes, both of them speak English

Point to yourself and one student, and ask

Are both of us speaking English?

Yes, both of us are speaking English

Are we both sitting?

No, we aren't both sitting; I'm sitting, but you're standing

mean	hello	goodbye	thank you

Explain that **The word "hello" means "..." in ...** (students' language). **The word "goodbye" means "..." in ...** (students' language). **The words "thank you" mean "..." in ...** (students' language).

What does the word "hello" mean in ...?

The word "hello" means "..." in ...

What does the word "goodbye" mean in ...?

The word "goodbye" means "..." in ...

What do the words "thank you" mean in ...?

The words "thank you" mean "..." in ...

67

language	European	Asian	Germany

Which language are we speaking now?

We're speaking English now

Which language do you generally speak?

I generally speak ...

Which language does he/she generally speak?

He/she generally speaks ...

Is Chinese a European language?

No, Chinese isn't a European language; it's an Asian language

Is Germany an Asian country?

No, Germany isn't an Asian country; it's a European country

Students read Lesson 8 on page 41

I	have not	I	haven't
you	have not	you	haven't
he	has not	he	hasn't
she	has not	she	hasn't
it	has not	it	hasn't
we	have not	we	haven't
you	have not	you	haven't
they	have not	they	haven't

only

The negative of "I have" is "I have not", and the contraction is "I haven't".

What's the negative of "I have"?

The negative of
"I have" is "I have not"

What's the contraction of "I have not"?

The contraction
of "I have not" is "I haven't"

Have I got four arms?

No, you haven't got four arms;
you've only got two arms

Have you got two heads?

No, I haven't got two heads;
I've only got one head

Has he only got one hand?

No, he hasn't only got one
hand; he's got two hands

Has she got two noses?

No, she hasn't got two noses;
she's only got one nose

Have we only got one mouth?

No, we haven't only
got one mouth; we've got
two mouths (i.e. you and the student)

Point to Mr and Mrs Brown, and ask

Have they got eight ears?

No, they haven't got eight ears;
they've only got four ears

the same ... as   different ... from   Japan

This book's the same as this book, but that book's different from this book.

Are your shoes the same as my shoes?

No, my shoes aren't
the same as your shoes;
they're different from your shoes

Are the French the same as the Russians?

No, the French
aren't the same as the Russians;
they're different from the Russians

Stress the article "the", and also the article "a" in the next two answers.

Are your eyes the same colour as my eyes?

Yes, my eyes are the same colour as your eyes ~
No, my eyes aren't the same colour as your eyes; they're a different colour from your eyes

Do the people in Germany speak the same language as the people in Japan?

No, the people in Germany don't speak the same language as the people in Japan; they speak a different language from the people in Japan

Which is it right to say: "people are" or "people is"?

It's right to say "people are"

 *Dictation 3*

Who are they?/ They're Mr and Mrs Long./ The plural of "man"/ is "men"./ The plural of "woman"/ is "women"./ The boots are/ under that chair./ These windows are red and blue;/ those are yellow and grey./ Sixteen, seventeen, eighteen,/ nineteen, twenty./ The letters/ of the alphabet/ are: ABC – DEF – GHI – JKL – MNO – PQR – STU – VWX – YZ./ A is before B/ and J is after I./ E is between/ D and F.

LESSON 13

 *See Chart 4*

anybody? non-specific	**somebody** **not anybody**
who? specific	**Mrs Brown** **Mr Smith etc.** **nobody**

Show the students the Chart and explain that **Both "anybody" and "somebody" mean "...". We use "anybody" in questions and negative sentences, and "somebody" in positive sentences. For example, we say "Is there anybody sitting here? Yes, there's somebody sitting here. Is there anybody sitting there? No, there isn't anybody sitting there"**. Also explain that **"Anybody" is non-specific and has a non-specific answer, whereas "who" is specific and has a specific answer – "Mrs Brown", "Mr Smith" etc., or "nobody"**.

What do the words "anybody" and "somebody" mean?

The words "anybody" and "somebody" mean ...

What's the difference between "anybody" and "somebody"?

The difference between "anybody" and "somebody" is that we use "anybody" in questions and negative sentences, whereas we use "somebody" in positive sentences

anybody

Is there anybody in this room?

Yes, there's somebody in this room

Is there anybody speaking to you?

Yes, there's somebody speaking to me

Is there anybody sitting there on that chair?

Yes, there's somebody sitting there on that chair

not anybody   corridor

Is there anybody sitting on the floor?

No, there isn't anybody sitting on the floor

Is there anybody in this room wearing a hat?

No, there isn't anybody in this room wearing a hat

Is there anybody in the corridor?

No, there isn't anybody in the corridor

nobody

Who's speaking English in this room?

We're speaking English in this room

Who's speaking (French) in this room?

Nobody's speaking (French) in this room

Who's wearing clothes in this room?

We're wearing clothes in this room

Who's wearing a hat in this room?

Nobody's wearing a hat in this room

Who's giving you an English lesson?

You're giving me an English lesson

Who's in the corridor?

Nobody's in the corridor

walk

Explain that **I'm walking. I'm walking to the window**. As you say the word "walking", move your first two fingers in a walking fashion.

What am I doing?	You're walking
Where am I walking to?	You're walking to the window
Do you like walking?	Yes, I like walking
Does he/she like walking?	Yes, he/she likes walking

 Students read Lesson 9 on page 48

Mr Brown's

Point to Chart 1, and say **This is the suit of Mr Brown, or this is Mr Brown's suit. We prefer to say "Mr Brown's suit" and not "the suit of Mr Brown"**. Next, point to Mrs Brown's dress, then to Mr Brown, and ask

Is this Mr Brown's dress?	No, it isn't Mr Brown's dress; it's Mrs Brown's dress
Is this Mr Brown's shirt?	Yes, it's Mr Brown's shirt

Point to Mrs Brown's arm, and ask

Is this Mr Brown's arm?	No, it isn't Mr Brown's arm; it's Mrs Brown's arm

Point to Mr Brown's ear, and ask

Is this Mr Smith's ear?	No, it isn't Mr Smith's ear; it's Mr Brown's ear

Continue practising the possessive apostrophe using the students' own names and clothing/possessions. For example, "Is this Maria's book? No, it isn't Maria's book; it's Paulo's book".

Is this ...'s book?

No, it isn't ...'s book; it's ...'s book

stand up   sit down   up   down

With the appropriate actions, explain that **I'm sitting down. I'm standing up. My right hand's moving up and down**.

What's my right hand doing?

Your right hand's moving up and down

What am I doing?

You're sitting down

What am I doing?

You're standing up

Do you sit down after the lesson?

No, I don't sit down after the lesson; I stand up after the lesson

cannot   can't

The negative of "can" is "cannot", and the contraction of "cannot" is "can't".

What's the negative of "can"?

The negative of "can" is "cannot"

What's the contraction of "cannot"?

The contraction of "cannot" is "can't"

Can you speak (Chinese)?

No, I can't speak (Chinese)

Can you put the table into your pocket?

No, I can't put the table into my pocket

Can you touch the ceiling?

No, I can't touch the ceiling

quarter

One is a quarter of four. Ten's a quarter of forty.

How much is a quarter of forty?

Ten is a quarter of forty

How much is a quarter of a thousand?

250 is a quarter
of a thousand

What's a quarter of ten?

Two-and-a-half is a
quarter of ten

What's a quarter of five?

One-and-a-quarter is a
quarter of five

teach   learn   Spanish

I'm teaching you English, and you're learning English from me.

Are you teaching me English?

No, I'm not teaching you
English; I'm learning English from you

Do you learn Spanish?

No, I don't learn Spanish; I learn English

Do you like learning a language?

Yes, I like
learning a language

Does he/she like learning a language?

Yes, he/she likes
learning a language

LESSON 14

easy	difficult	grammar

Is English grammar difficult?

> No, English grammar isn't difficult; it's easy

Is Chinese an easy language to learn?

> No, Chinese isn't an easy language to learn; it's a difficult language to learn

Is it difficult for you to speak your language?

> No, it isn't difficult for me to speak my language; it's easy

Is it generally easy for people to write with their left hand?

> No, it isn't generally easy for people to write with their left hand; it's difficult

hang	map

What's my pen doing?

> Your pen's hanging between your finger and your thumb

Is there a light hanging from the ceiling?

> Yes, there's a light hanging from the ceiling ~ No, there isn't a light hanging from the ceiling

Is there a map hanging on that wall?

> Yes, there's a map hanging on that wall ~ No, there isn't a map hanging on that wall

by   car   bus   train   school

Do you go home after the lesson by car, by bus, by train or do you walk home?

I go home after the lesson by ...
~ I walk home after the lesson;
I don't go by car, by bus or by train

Which do you prefer: to walk or go by car?

I prefer to ...

Do you come to school by train or by bus?

I come to school by ...

Does he/she come to school by train or by bus?

He/She comes to school by ...

married   single   Miss

Are you married?

Yes, I'm married ~ No, I'm not married; I'm single

Is Mr Brown single?

No, Mr Brown isn't single; he's married

Is Miss Brown married?

No, Miss Brown isn't married; she's single

 Students read Lesson 10 on page 53

husband   wife

Has Mr Brown got a wife?

Yes, Mr Brown's got a wife

Has Mrs Brown got a husband?

Yes, Mrs Brown's got a husband

Is Mrs Brown's husband standing behind the house?

No, Mrs Brown's husband isn't standing behind the house; he's standing in front of the house

mother   father

What's your mother's name?

My mother's name is …

What's your father's name?

My father's name is …

What's your father's wife's name?

My father's wife's name is …

What's your mother's husband's name?

My mother's husband's name is …

Explain, if necessary, that your father's wife is your mother and that your mother's husband is your father. If such questions are too complicated leave them out.

child   children   only child

The plural of "child" is "children".

What's the plural of "child"?

The plural of "child" is "children"

How many children have your mother and father got?

My mother and father have got … child/children

Are you an only child?

Yes, I'm an only child ~ No, I'm not an only child

call   mum   dad

Touch your body and your clothes etc., and explain that **We call this a mouth, we call this a tie etc.** Then explain that **People generally call their mother and father "Mum" and "Dad"**.

What do we call this?

We call this an arm (or a handkerchief, a leg etc.)

Select about three or four things.

What do we call the people in France?

We call the people in France French

What do we call the thing we wear on our heads?

We call the thing we wear on our heads a hat

What do people generally call their mother and father?

People generally call their mother and father "Mum" and "Dad"

one ... the other

Put one hand on the table and the other on your arm, and say **Both my hands aren't on the table; one's on the table and the other's on my arm**.

Are both my hands on the table?

No, both your hands aren't on the table; one's on the table and the other's on your arm

Are both my hands closed?

No, both your hands aren't closed; one's closed and the other's open

Are both these pencils red?

No, both these pencils aren't red; one's red and the other's grey

kind

What's this?

It's a book

What kind of book is this?

It's an English book

What kind of room is this?

It's a classroom

What kind of car do you prefer?

I prefer ...

 *Dictation 4*

We are/ in front of them,/ and they are/ behind us./ There are/ five vowels/ in the English alphabet:/ A, E, I, O, U./ I'm the teacher/ and you're the student./ Thirty, forty, fifty,/ sixty, seventy,/ eighty, ninety,/ a hundred, a thousand,/ a million./ Thirty plus thirteen/ equals forty-three./ There's a shoe/ on the floor./ This is/ not a sock/ or a jacket;/ it's a suit./ Now put the book here,/ please.

 *Do Revision Exercise 2*

LESSON 15

Preposition

The words "on", "under", "in", "from" etc. are prepositions.

Give me some examples of prepositions, please.

> Some examples of prepositions are "on", "under", "in" and "from"

Where do you come from?

> I come from ...

Where do I come from?

> You come from ...

Explain that **When we use question words, for example "what", "which" and "where", we put the preposition last in the sentence. For example, we do not say "From where do you come?"; we say "Where do you come from?" We do not say "On what are you putting the book?"; we say "What are you putting the book on?"**

Do not confuse the students at this stage by telling them that, in formal written English, the preposition is often placed before the question word.

What do we speak with?

> We speak with our mouths

Where am I taking the book from?

> You're taking the book from the table

What am I putting the pen under?

> You're putting the pen under the book

What are you sitting on?

> I'm sitting on a chair

north   south   east   west

cardinal point   Paris

North, south, east and west are the four cardinal points. Explain what you mean on a map on the wall. If there is no map, then point in the air with your finger at the four points of the compass, or translate.

Tell me the names of the four cardinal points, please.

The names of the four cardinal points are north, south, east and west

Is Greece west of Italy?

No, Greece isn't west of Italy; it's east of Italy

Is Paris in the south of France?

No, Paris isn't in the south of France; it's in the north of France

Is Germany east or west of Italy?

Germany isn't east or west of Italy; it's north of Italy

place   some of

How many places are there in this room?

There are ... places in this room

Is there anybody sitting in that place?

Yes, there's somebody sitting in that place

Tell me the names of some of the places you like in this country?

The names of some of the places I like in this country are ...

 *Students read Lesson 11 on page 62*

opposite

Mime clearly as you explain that **The opposite of "long" is "short". The opposite of "large" is "small".**

What's the opposite of "high"?

The opposite of "high" is "low"

What's the opposite of "behind"?

The opposite of "behind" is "in front of"

What's the opposite of "tall"?

The opposite of "tall" is "short"

What's the opposite of the verb "to teach"?

The opposite of the verb "to teach" is "to learn"

without

The opposite of "with" is "without". We can write with a pen or a pencil, but we can't write without a pen or a pencil. Each time you say the word "without" you could accompany it with the placing of your hands crossways, one on top of the other, palms downwards, and then with a rapid sideways movement cut the air with them. All such movements help to keep the students' attention on you.

What's the opposite of "with"?

The opposite of "with" is "without"

Can we write without a pen or a pencil?

No, we can't write without a pen or a pencil

Can we speak without opening our mouths?

No, we can't speak without opening our mouths

Can you read without wearing glasses?

Yes, I can read without wearing glasses ~ No, I can't read without wearing glasses

__Verb__   __Noun__   translation

A verb is a word we use for an action. For example, "take", "put", "open", "close" etc. are verbs. A noun is the name of a thing. For example, "book", "picture", "wall" etc. are nouns. The word "translate" is a verb, whereas the word "translation" is a noun. The word "mean" is a verb, whereas the word "meaning" is a noun.

What's the difference between a verb and a noun?

> The difference between a verb and a noun is that a verb is a word we use for an action, whereas a noun is the name of a thing

Give me an example of a verb, please.

> "Take" is a verb

Give me an example of a noun.

> "Book" is a noun

Is the word "translation" a verb or a noun?

> The word "translation" is a noun

during   **about**

Do we speak ... during the lesson?

> No, we don't speak ... during the lesson; we speak English

Do you walk about the room during the lesson?

> No, I don't walk about the room during the lesson; I sit on my chair

Does he/she walk about the room during the lesson?

> No, he/she doesn't walk about the room during the lesson; he/she sits on his/her chair

About how many questions do you answer during the lesson?

> I answer about ... questions during the lesson

LESSON 16

some ... some

Are all the people in this town (or city or village) men?

> No, not all the people in this town are men; some are men and some are women

Are all the cars in Europe Fords?

> No, not all the cars in Europe are Fords; some are Fords and some are Fiats, Renaults, Volkswagens, Volvos etc.

Are all the people in this place married?

> No, not all the people in this place are married; some are married and some are single

Do all the people in Europe speak Spanish?

> No, not all the people in Europe speak Spanish; some speak Spanish and some speak other languages

 See Chart 4

anything?	**something**
non-specific	**not anything**
what?	a light
specific	a picture
	nothing

Show the students Chart 4, and explain that **"Anything" and "something" both mean the same thing. We use "anything" in questions and negative sentences, and we use "something" in positive sentences. For example, we say "Have I got anything in my right hand? Yes, you've got something in your right hand. Have I got anything in my left hand? No, you haven't got anything in your left hand."** Also explain that **"Anything" we use in a non-specific question, whereas "What?" is specific and has a specific answer – "a light, a book" etc., or "nothing"**. It may not be necessary to explain all this, as it is the same as for "any" and "anybody" and should be evident from the Chart. How much you explain will depend on the ability of the students to understand.

anything

Have I got anything in my right hand?

Yes, you've got something in your right hand

Is there anything on the table?

Yes, there's something on the table

Are you wearing anything on your feet?

Yes, I'm wearing something on my feet

not anything

Have I got anything in my left hand?

No, you haven't got anything in your left hand

Is there anything there on the floor?

No, there isn't anything there on the floor

Are you wearing anything on your head?

No, I'm not wearing anything on my head

Students read Lesson 12 on page 66

nothing

What have I got in my right hand?

You've got a pen in
your right hand

What have I got in my left hand?

You've got nothing in
your left hand

What's on the table?

There are some books, some pens etc.
on the table (stress the word "some")

What's there on the floor?

There's nothing there
on the floor

What are you wearing on your feet?

I'm wearing shoes on
my feet

What are you wearing on your head?

I'm wearing nothing
on my head

Only one negative

In English, in a negative sentence, we use only <u>one</u> negative word, not two. For example, **we say** (point to an empty chair) **"There is<u>n't</u> anything on this chair". A sentence with two negative words has a positive meaning. For example, "There isn't <u>nobody</u> on this chair"** means that there <u>is somebody</u> on the chair. **"I have <u>not</u> got <u>nothing</u> in my pocket"** means that I <u>have</u> got <u>something</u> in my pocket.

Have I got anything in my hand?

Yes, you've got
something in your hand

Have I got nothing in my hand?

No, you haven't got nothing
in your hand; you've got
something in your hand

What does this sentence mean: "I'm <u>not</u> eating <u>nothing</u>"?

"I'm not eating nothing" means
"I'm eating something"

front   back   top   bottom   side

Take a book, and say **This is the front of the book. This is the back of the book. This is the top of the book. This is the bottom of the book. And this is the side of the book**. Then repeat **"front", "back", "top", "bottom", "side"**. If necessary, repeat the same process using your head in place of the book. Use the complete sentence for each word, i.e. **This is the ... of the book** etc., as it gives the students time to think and ponder on the new word.

What part of the book is this?

It's the front (back, top, bottom, side) of the book

Is this the front part of my body?

No, it isn't the front part of your body; it's the back part of your body

Balance a pen on the top of a book, and ask

Where's the pen?

The pen's on the top of the book

What's on the top of my head?

Your hair's on the top of your head

Are my ears on the back of my head?

No, your ears aren't on the back of your head; they're on the sides of your head

Are you sitting on my left-hand side or on my right-hand side?

I'm sitting on your ...

smell

What am I doing?

You're smelling your wrist

What do we smell with?

We smell with our noses

Has the table got any smell?

No, the table hasn't got any smell

address   street

The address of this school is 137 High Street, (and then the name of the town).

What's the address of this school?

The address of this
school is ... Street

What's your address?

My address is ... Street

 *Dictation 5*

The capital of England/ is not a town/ but a city./ Greece, Italy and France/ are in Europe,/ and China and India/ are in Asia./ Moscow's the capital of Russia,/ not Athens./ How much is/ thirty plus fifteen?/ There are a number of shirts,/ ties and hats/ in this room./ Those are her tights./ The cardinal numbers are/ one, two, three etc./ This is my coat.

LESSON 17

| many | few | match | matchbox |

Are there many people in a small village?

No, there aren't many people in a small village; there are few people in a small village

Are there few people in a large city?

No, there aren't few people in a large city; there are many people in a large city

Have you and I got many pens?

No, you and I haven't got many pens; we've got few pens

Are there few matches in a matchbox?

No, there aren't few matches in a matchbox; there are many matches in a matchbox

| friend | friendly |

Have you got any friends?

Yes, I've got some friends

Do you think the people in your town are friendly?

Yes, I think the people in my town are friendly ~ No, I don't think the people in my town are friendly; they're unfriendly

Are the countries of Europe generally friends now?

Yes, the countries of Europe are generally friends now

into   in   that   another

I'm putting my pen into my pocket. My pen is in my pocket. I'm coming into the room. I'm in the room now. We use "into" for a thing that moves from one place to another, and "in" for a thing that remains in one place.

What am I doing?

> You're putting your pen into your pocket

Where's my pen now?

> Your pen's in your pocket now

Go out of the classroom, and, as you come back in, ask

What am I doing?

> You're coming into the classroom

Where am I now?

> You're in the classroom now

What's the difference between "into" and "in"?

> The difference between "into" and "in" is that we use "into" for a thing that moves from one place to another, and "in" for a thing that remains in one place

see   such as

What can you see in this room?

> I can see many things in this room, such as some students, a table, a clock ...

Can you see him/her?

> Yes, I can see him/her

Can you see anything in my left hand?

> No, I can't see anything in your left hand

 Students read Lesson 13 on page 71

why   because   similar   too   Greenwich

"Why" and "because" have similar meanings, but we generally use "why" in questions and "because" in answers. Translate "too" if necessary in the following answers.

What's the difference between "why" and "because"?

The difference between "why" and "because" is that we generally use "why" in questions and "because" in answers

Can you touch the ceiling?

No, I can't touch the ceiling

Why not?

Because the ceiling's too high for me to touch

Can you put this book into your pocket?

No, I can't put that book into my pocket

Why not?

Because that book's too large to go into my pocket

Can we call Grantchester (in England) a city?

No, we can't call Grantchester (in England) a city

Why not?

Because Grantchester is too small for us to call a city; Grantchester is a village

second   minute   hour   make

Sixty seconds make a minute. Sixty minutes make an hour.

How many seconds make a minute?

Sixty seconds make a minute

How many minutes make an hour?

Sixty minutes make an hour

Can you make a suit?

Yes, I can make a suit ~ No, I can't make a suit

Adjective

The words "black", "white", "large", "small", "high", "low" etc. are adjectives. In English, we put adjectives before nouns.

Give me some examples of adjectives, please.

> Some examples of adjectives are black, white, large ...

Is the word "book" an adjective?

> No, the word "book" isn't an adjective; it's a noun

Which word is the adjective in this sentence: "The green pen is on the floor"?

> The word "green" is the adjective in this sentence

In English, do we put an adjective before or after a noun?

> In English, we put an adjective before a noun.

Give me an example, please.

> a blue book; a high ceiling; an easy language

LESSON 18

food

Do you like food?

Yes, I like food

Do you like all food?

Yes, I like all food ~ No, I don't like all food; some I like and some I dislike

Do people generally dislike the smell of food?

No, people don't generally dislike the smell of food; they like the smell of food

son   daughter

How many sons has your dad got?

My dad's got ... son(s)

How many daughters has your mum got?

My mum's got ... daughter(s)

Are you a son or a daughter?

I'm a ...

brother   sister

Have you got any brothers?

Yes, I've got a/some brother(s) ~ No, I haven't got any brothers

Have you got any sisters?

Yes, I've got a/some sister(s) ~ No, I haven't got any sisters

How many brothers and sisters have you got?

I've got ...

parents   **relatives**   **relations**   **family**

uncle   **aunt**   **cousin**

Parents are mother and father, whereas relatives are all the other people in the family, such as brothers, sisters, uncles, aunts, cousins etc. Another word for "relatives" is "relations".

What's the difference between parents and relatives?

The difference between parents and relatives is that parents are mother and father, whereas relatives are all the other people in the family, such as brothers, sisters, uncles, aunts, cousins etc.

What does the word "uncle" mean?

The word "uncle" means your mother's brother, or your father's brother

What does the word "aunt" mean?

The word "aunt" means your mother's sister, or your father's sister

What does the word "cousin" mean?

The word "cousin" means your uncle's child, or your aunt's child

more ... than

Hold up your hands, and say **I've got eight fingers and two thumbs on my hands. I've got more fingers than thumbs on my hands**. Then ask

Have you got more fingers than thumbs on your hands?

Yes, I've got more fingers than thumbs on my hands

Are there more people in a town than in a village?

Yes, there are more people in a town than in a village

Are there more pages in this book than in that book?

Yes, there are more pages in this book than in that book

 *Students read Lesson 14 on page 76*

break

Pretend to break your pen.

What am I doing?

You're breaking your pen

Can you break the window with a chair?

Yes, I can break the window with a chair

Can you break the table with your hands?

No, I can't break the table with my hands

out of

I'm putting my pen into my pocket. My pen is in my pocket. I'm taking my pen out of my pocket. I'm coming into the room. I'm in the room. I'm going out of the room. Repeat the words **"into", "in", "out of"**.

What am I doing?

You're putting your pen into your pocket

What am I doing?

You're taking your pen out of your pocket

What am I doing?

You're going out of the classroom

What am I doing?

You're coming into the classroom

What am I doing?

You're putting your hands into your pockets

What am I doing?

You're taking your hands out of your pockets

Do you go out of the classroom before the lesson?

No, I don't go out of the classroom before the lesson; I come into the classroom before the lesson

think

When asking a question with the word "think", tap your head with your forefinger.

About how many people do you think there are in France (or Italy etc.)?

I think there are about ... people in ...

Do you think there's anybody in the other room?

Yes, I think there's somebody in the other room ~ No I don't think there's anybody in the other room

What do you think I've got in my pocket?

I think you've got ... in your pocket

good   bad   good at   bad at

Is this a bad pen?

No, it isn't a bad pen; it's a good pen

Do you think that's a good picture?

Yes, I think that's a good picture ~ No, I don't think that's a good picture; I think it's a bad picture

Are all children good children?

No, not all children are good children; some are good and some are bad

Are all students good at learning languages?

No, not all students are good at learning languages; some are good at learning languages and some are bad at learning languages

instead of

Do you prefer tea instead of coffee? Yes, I prefer tea instead of coffee ~ No, I don't prefer tea instead of coffee; I prefer coffee instead of tea

Do you prefer coming to school instead of going to the cinema? No, I don't prefer coming to school instead of going to the cinema; I prefer going to the cinema instead of coming to school

Do you prefer walking instead of going by car? Yes, I prefer walking instead of going by car ~ No, I don't prefer walking instead of going by car; I prefer going by car instead of walking

 *Dictation 6*

We're reading,/ not writing./ That's his pullover/ and these are/ her tights./ These are/ our skirts./ Those are/ their trousers./ Your handkerchief/ is in/ your pocket./ Her blouse is grey./ Miss Smith/ is not French/ or German;/ she's English./ Give me/ the last match/ in your hand./ We say/ one person,/ but two people./ He's coming from London/ and going to Beijing./ This is my finger,/ not my thumb.

 *Do Revision Exercise 3*

LESSON 19

bread   butter   rice

Pretend to spread butter on the palm of one hand with the index finger of the other hand.

What do we put on our bread?
We put butter on our bread

Do you like bread without butter?
Yes, I like bread without butter ~ No, I don't like bread without butter; I only like bread with butter

What colour's butter?
Butter's yellow or white

Do you prefer white or brown rice?
I prefer ... rice

carry

Pick up your chair, walk to the window with it, and say **I'm carrying my chair to the window**.

What am I doing?
You're carrying your chair to the window

Do you think you can carry this table on your back?
Yes, I think I can carry this table on my back ~ No, I don't think I can carry this table on my back

Am I carrying a tie (or dress etc.)?
No, you aren't carrying a tie; you're wearing a tie

Am I wearing a handkerchief?
No, you aren't wearing a handkerchief; you're carrying a handkerchief

no = not any

**The word "no" can mean "not any". For example, we can say "I have <u>not</u> got <u>any</u> books"
or "I have got <u>no</u> books"; the sentences have the same meaning.**

What can we say instead of "not any books"?

We can say "no books" instead of "not any books"

Give me another example, please.

"They haven't got any friends" or "They have no friends"

hear

Cup your hand around your ear.

Can you hear me speaking to you?

Yes, I can hear you speaking to me

Can you hear anybody in the other room?

Yes, I can hear somebody in the other room ~ No, I can't hear anybody in the other room

Point to your ear.

What do we hear with?

We hear with our ears

drive

Move your hands as if you were driving a car.

Can you drive a car?

Yes, I can drive a car ~ No, I can't drive a car

Is there anybody in your family who can't drive a car?

Yes, there's somebody in my family who can't drive a car ~ No, there isn't anybody in my family who can't drive a car

money	**pence**	**pound**

How much money have you got in your pocket (or bag)?

> I've got about ... in my pocket (or bag)

How many pence make a pound?

> A hundred pence
> make a pound

How many euros (or dollars etc.) make a pound?

> About ... euros (or dollars etc.) make a pound

 Students read Lesson 15 on page 81

fewer ... than

For the words "more" and "fewer", as you ask the question and the student answers, put both hands out level (palms down); for "more", raise one hand higher than the other, and for "fewer" or "less", lower it below the level of the other.

I've got two thumbs and eight fingers on my hands. I've got fewer thumbs than fingers on my hands.

Have I got more thumbs than fingers on my hands?

> No, you haven't got more thumbs
> than fingers on your hands; you've got
> fewer thumbs than fingers on your hands

Are there more pages in this book than in that book?

> No, there aren't more pages in
> this book than in that book; there are
> fewer pages in this book than in that book

Are there more people in Europe than in Asia?

> No, there aren't more people
> in Europe than in Asia; there are
> fewer people in Europe than in Asia

Are there more tables in this school than chairs?

No, there aren't more tables in
this school than chairs; there are
fewer tables in this school than chairs

watch

The difference between a watch and a clock is that we wear a watch on our wrist, whereas we hang a clock on the wall or put it on a table.

What's the difference between a watch and a clock?

The difference between a watch and a clock is that
we wear a watch on our wrist, whereas we hang a
clock on the wall or put it on a table

The difference between "wear" and "carry" is that we use "wear" for a thing that is on the body, whereas we use "carry" for a thing that is not on the body. For example, I am wearing my watch on my wrist, but when I put it into my pocket, I am carrying it.

What's the difference between "wear" and "carry"?

The difference between "wear" and "carry"
is that we use "wear" for a thing that is on the body,
whereas we use "carry" for a thing that is not on the body

Is there a clock in this room?

Yes, there's a clock in this
room ~ No, there isn't a clock in this room

Am I carrying a watch?

No, you aren't carrying a watch;
you're wearing a watch

What are you carrying in your pocket (or bag)?

I'm carrying ... in my pocket (or bag)

LESSON 20

 *See Chart 6*

| time | past | to | by | o'clock |

Go through all the clocks, asking

What's the time by this clock?   It's 3 o'clock etc.

What's the time now, please?   It's ... now

With the numbers 5, 10, 20, and 25 we don't say "minutes". For example, we say "It's 5 past 3." With the numbers between one and five, five and ten etc. we say "minutes". For example, "It's 2 minutes past 4."

| day | week | month | year |

60 seconds make a minute; 60 minutes make an hour; 24 hours make a day; 7 days make a week; 4 weeks make a month; 12 months make a year.

How many seconds make a minute?   60 seconds make a minute

How many minutes make an hour?   60 minutes make an hour

How many hours make a day?   24 hours make a day

How many days make a week?   7 days make a week

How many weeks make a month?   4 weeks make a month

How many months make a year?   12 months make a year

also

Give me an example of the word "also", please.

I can speak my language and I can also speak English

meat   sugar

Do you like meat?   Yes, I like meat ~ No, I don't like meat

What colour's sugar?   Sugar's white or brown

Do you put sugar on your meat?   No, I don't put sugar
on my meat; I put it in my tea or coffee

count   from ... to

1, 2, 3, 4, 5. I'm counting.

1, 2, 3, 4, 5 – What am I doing?   You're counting

6, 7, 8, 9, 10. I'm counting the numbers from six to ten.

6, 7, 8, 9, 10 – What am I doing?   You're counting the
numbers from six to ten

Count the numbers from 100 to 105, please.   One hundred,
one hundred and one,
one hundred and two ...

What's he/she doing?   He/She's counting the
numbers from 100 to 105

 Students read Lesson 16 on page 85

Possessive adjectives	**Possessive pronouns**
my	mine
your	yours
his	his
her	hers
its	–
our	ours
your	yours
their	theirs

The possessive adjectives are "my", "your", "his", "her", "its", "our", "your", "their", whereas the possessive pronouns are "mine", "yours", "his", "hers", "ours", "yours", "theirs". Stress the "s" at the end of the possessive pronouns.

What are the possessive adjectives?

The possessive adjectives are "my", "your" ...

What are the possessive pronouns?

The possessive pronouns are "mine", "yours" ...

The difference between a possessive adjective and a possessive pronoun is that we put a possessive adjective in front of a noun (for example, "This is my book"), whereas we use a possessive pronoun instead of a noun. For example, instead of saying "This is my pen and that is her pen", we can say "This is my pen and that is hers".

What's the difference between a possessive adjective and a possessive pronoun?

The difference between a possessive adjective and a possessive pronoun is that we put a possessive adjective in front of a noun whereas we use a possessive pronoun instead of a noun

Give me an example, please.

This is my book. This book is mine. This is mine.

mine   ## yours

Is this your ear?

No, that isn't my ear; it's your ear

Is this ear yours?

No, that ear isn't mine; it's yours

Is that nose mine?

No, this nose isn't yours; it's mine

See Chart 1 or point to other students

his   ## hers

Point to Mrs Brown's dress, then to Mr Brown, and ask

Is that dress his?

No, that dress isn't his; it's hers

Is that suit hers?

No, that suit isn't hers; it's his

Are those hands his?

No, those hands aren't his; they're hers

Are those arms hers?

No, those arms aren't hers; they're his

ours   ## theirs

Point to Mr and Mrs Brown's legs, and ask

Are those legs ours?

No, those legs aren't ours; they're theirs

Point to your book and the student's book, and then to Mr and Mrs Brown, and ask

Are these their books?

No, these aren't their books; they're our books

Are these books theirs?

No, these books aren't theirs;
they're ours

Infinitive

Verbs in the infinitive generally have the word "to" in front of them. For example, "to do", "to come", "to go" etc.

Give me some examples of verbs in the infinitive, please.

Some examples of verbs in the infinitive are
"to come", "to go", "to take" etc.

Auxiliary verb   do

An auxiliary verb is part of the verb in a sentence, but it does not tell us the action. For example, in the sentence "We are speaking", the word "speaking" tells us the action, and the word "are" is an auxiliary verb. In the sentence "He can read", the word "can" is the auxiliary verb. The auxiliary verb for the present simple is "do". For example, we say "Do you speak English?" or "I do not have a bag".

Which word is the auxiliary verb in this sentence: "They can open the window"?

The word "can" is the auxiliary
verb in that sentence

Which word is the auxiliary verb in this sentence: "Do they walk to school?"

The word "do" is the auxiliary
verb in that sentence

Also, the word "do" means (translate into student's language). **For example, "What is he doing?" – "He's sitting on a chair".**

What does the verb "to do" mean?

The verb "to do" means ...

What am I doing?

You're going out of the room

What do I do after the lesson?

You go out of the room after
the lesson

What am I doing?	You're sitting down
What do you do before the lesson?	I sit down before the lesson
What am I doing?	You're standing up
What do you do after the lesson?	I stand up after the lesson

 Dictation 7

This part of the body/ is a leg/ and this/ is an arm./ The plural of "foot"/ is "feet"./ There are twelve words/ in this sentence./ A verb is a word/ we use for an action./ What does the word/ "do" mean?/ As an auxiliary verb/ it means nothing./ We say "the book",/ but "the umbrella"./ Question mark, full stop,/ comma./ The letter A/ isn't a consonant,/ but a vowel./ This answer is wrong./ That is right.

LESSON 21

the most

Take three books, each with a different number of pages. Then, referring to each one in turn, say **This book** (the thickest book) **has more pages than this book** (the second thickest book), **and this book** (the second thickest book) **has more pages than this book** (the thinnest book). **This book** (the thickest book) **has the most pages**.

Of these three books, which book has the most pages?

> Of these three books,
> this book has the most pages

Which city in this country has the most people?

> ... is the
> city in this country which has the most people

Which person in your family reads the most books?

> My ... is the person in my
> family who reads the most books

Which school in this town has the most students?

> ... is the school in this town
> which has the most students

beautiful   handsome   ugly

Do you think Paris is an ugly city?

> No, I don't think Paris
> is an ugly city; I think it's a beautiful city

Do you think ... is a beautiful place?

> No, I don't think ... is a
> beautiful place; I think it's an ugly place

Insert into the above question the name of an ugly place known to the students.

Do you think (use here the name of a film star) is ugly?

> No, I don't
> think ... is ugly; I think she's beautiful/he's handsome

Which do you think's the most beautiful place in this country?

I think ... is the most
beautiful place in this country

eat

For the word "eat", pretend to put a small piece of bread into your mouth and chew it, or pretend to eat with a knife and fork.

What am I doing?

You're eating

Do you eat all food?

No, I don't eat all food; some I eat and some I don't eat

Do you eat bread without butter?

Yes, I eat bread without butter ~ No, I don't eat bread without butter

Point to your mouth.

What do we eat with?

We eat with our mouths

drink   water   wine   milk

The names of some drinks are "water", "wine" and "milk".

Pretend to drink something.

What am I doing?

You're drinking

Do you drink tea?

Yes, I drink tea ~ No, I don't drink tea

Can we drink meat?

No, we can't drink meat; we eat meat

For the following question, to prevent the students answering with "tea", "coffee", "whisky" etc., give them the words for "water" etc. in their own language and ask them to translate. In the answer to the second question, stress the word "no".

Tell me the names of some drinks, please.

The names of some drinks are water, wine and milk

What colour's water?

Water has no colour

Is there a drink on the table?

Yes there's a drink on the table ~ No, there isn't a drink on the table

Do you drink wine?

Yes, I drink wine ~ No, I don't drink wine

Which drink do you prefer: milk or water?

I prefer ...

metal   gold   silver   steel   iron

The names of four metals are "gold", "silver", "steel" and "iron".

Tell me the names of four metals, please.

The names of four metals are gold, silver, steel and iron

 *Students read Lesson 17 on page 90*

made of   key   plastic

My watch is made of gold. A key is generally made of steel. For the word "key", point to the door and pretend to be turning a key.

Is your watch made of plastic?

Yes, my watch is made of plastic ~ No, my watch isn't made of plastic; it's made of ...

What's a key generally made of?

A key's generally made of steel

Are you wearing anything made of silver?

Yes, I'm wearing something made of silver ~ No, I'm not wearing anything made of silver

cost

How much do you think this pen costs?

I think that pen costs about ...

Do your shoes cost more than your handkerchief?

Yes, my shoes cost more than my handkerchief

How much does the cinema cost in this town?

The cinema costs about ... in this town

like

The word "like" means "similar to". For example, this book is like this book here, but this book is different from that book there. The word "like" also means "such as". For example, I eat different kinds of food, like Chinese, Indian, Spanish etc.

What does the word "like" mean (not the verb)?

The word "like" means "similar to" or "such as"

Is this book like that book?

Yes, this book is like that book

Is your face the same as your father's?

No, my face isn't the same as my father's; it's like my father's

Do you eat different kinds of food, like Chinese, Indian, Spanish etc.?

Yes, I eat different kinds of food, like Chinese, Indian, Spanish etc. ~ No, I don't eat different kinds of food, like Chinese, Indian, Spanish etc.

Monday	**Tuesday**	**Wednesday**
Thursday	**Friday**	**Saturday**
Sunday	**weekend**	

The days of the week are Monday ... etc. We call Saturday and Sunday the weekend.

Tell me the names of the days of the week, please.

The names of the days of the week are Monday,
Tuesday, Wednesday, Thursday, Friday,
Saturday and Sunday

Each student names a day. If one student cannot remember, move immediately on to the next. Go through the days twice.

What do we call Saturday and Sunday?

We call Saturday
and Sunday the weekend

today	yesterday	tomorrow
was	**will be**	**to be**

Today is (for example) **Wednesday. Yesterday was Tuesday. Tomorrow will be Thursday.** For the words "yesterday" and "was", wave your hand as if throwing something over your shoulder. For "tomorrow" and "will be", make a circular movement forward with your index finger. For "today" point downwards with your index finger.

What's today?
Today's ...

What was yesterday?
Yesterday was ...

What will tomorrow be?
Tomorrow will be ...

What will the day after tomorrow be?
The day after
tomorrow will be ...

What was the day before yesterday?
The day before
yesterday was ...

LESSON 22

want   at the moment

Accompany the word "break" with appropriate actions, and translate "want" as you go.

Do you want to break your pen?

> No, I don't want to
> break my pen

Do you want to break the window?

> No, I don't want to
> break the window

Do you want anything to eat at the moment?

> Yes, I want something to eat at the moment
> ~ No, I don't want anything to eat at the moment

Do you want anything to drink at the moment?

> Yes, I want something to drink at the moment ~
> No, I don't want anything to drink at the moment

do you have ...?   you don't have ...

Instead of using "got" with the verb "have", we can use the present simple auxiliary "do". We can say "Have you got a pen?" or "Do you have a pen?" We can say "You haven't got any money" or "You don't have any money". There is no difference.

Do you have anything in your pocket (or bag)?

> Yes, I have something in my pocket (or bag)

What do they have on their feet?

> They have shoes on
> their feet

Do you have any relatives in this town?

> Yes, I have some
> relatives in this town ~ No, I
> don't have any relatives in this town

begin   end   last   how long

The lesson begins at three o'clock and ends at ten to four. The lesson lasts 50 minutes.

At what time does the lesson begin?   The lesson begins at ...

At what time does the lesson end?   The lesson ends at ...

How long does the lesson last?   The lesson lasts ...

cheap   expensive   Rolls Royce

This pen costs ... . It's cheap. My watch (or a Rolls Royce) costs ... . It's expensive.

Is this pen expensive?   No, that pen isn't expensive; it's cheap

Is a Rolls Royce cheap?   No, a Rolls Royce isn't cheap;
           it's expensive

Is my handkerchief expensive?   No, your handkerchief isn't
           expensive; it's cheap

the fewest

As with "the most", take three books with a different number of pages, and say **This book has fewer pages than this book, and this book has fewer pages than this book. This book has the fewest pages**. Then, pointing to the thinnest book, ask

Of these three books, has this book got the most pages?
           No, of these three books, that book hasn't
           got the most pages; it's got the fewest pages

Which person in your family reads the fewest books?
           My ... is the person in my
           family who reads the fewest books

Of these three countries, Germany, France, and Greece, has Greece got the most people?

No, of those three countries, Greece hasn't got the most people; it's got the fewest people

 *Students read Lesson 18 on page 94*

building

About how many rooms are there in this building?

There are about ... rooms in this building

Is this building high (or low)?

No, this building isn't ... ; it's ...

inside   outside   stomach

Take a pencil-box, or some such container, and put your finger inside it, and say **This is the inside of the box**. Rub all round the outside with your finger and say **This is the outside of the box**. (Repeat the words **inside** and **outside**.)

What part of the box is this?

It's the inside of the box

What part of the box is this?

It's the outside of the box

What can you see outside this window?

I can see a building etc. outside this window

Are we sitting outside in the corridor?

No, we aren't sitting outside in the corridor; we're sitting inside the classroom

Is there any food inside our stomachs after eating?

Yes, there's some food inside our stomachs after eating

a   some

The plural of "a" is "some". For example, we say "a pen", but "some pens".

What's the plural of "a"?	The plural of "a" is "some"
What's the plural of "a book"?	The plural of "a book" is "some books"
What can you see in this classroom?	I can see some books, some pens, a teacher, a door etc. in this classroom
Have I got a thumb on my left hand?	Yes, you've got a thumb on your left hand
Have I got any fingers on my left hand?	Yes, you've got some fingers on your left hand

well

Can you hear well?	Yes, I can hear well
Can you see well?	Yes, I can see well
Can you speak ... well?	Yes, I can speak ... well

For the above question, fill in the space with the name of the student's own language.

flower   plant

Do you like the smell of flowers?	Yes, I like the smell of flowers
Have you got any plants at home?	Yes, I've got some plants at home ~ No, I haven't got any plants at home

whose

Whose book's this?   It's your book

Whose hand's that?   It's his/her hand

Whose suit's that?   It's Mr Brown's suit

love   hate

Do children generally love going to school?   No, children
                                    don't generally love going to
                            school; they generally hate going to school

Do children hate their mothers?   No, children don't hate
                            their mothers; they love their mothers

Do you love eating bad food?   No, I don't love eating bad
                                food; I hate eating bad food

Do you hate all food?   No, I don't hate all food; some I
                                    hate and some I love

 *Dictation 8*

What is the meaning/ of the word "wrist"?/ How many things/ are there here?/
Her hair/ is on her head./ His chin,/ mouth and nose/ are on his face./ My eyes
are blue./ The people of Scandinavia/ are tall./ He's asking us a question./ The
name of her country/ is Germany./ Who are you?/ The contraction/ of the verb "to
have"/ is "I've, you've, he's" etc./ Have you got any ears?/ Yes, two.

 *Do Revision Exercise 4*

LESSON 23

meal	breakfast	lunch

dinner	a day	morning	evening

People generally eat three meals a day, which we call breakfast, lunch and dinner. We generally have breakfast at about 8 o'clock in the morning, lunch at about one o'clock, and dinner at about 8 o'clock in the evening. There are other meals at other times, but the teacher should not comment on these at this stage of the students' studies.

Tell me the names of the three meals that people generally eat a day.
The names of the three meals that people generally eat a day are breakfast, lunch and dinner

What time do you have your breakfast?
I have my breakfast at ...

What time do you have your lunch?
I have my lunch at ...

What time does your dinner begin?
My dinner begins at ...

What time does your dinner end?
My dinner ends at ...

The above two questions are directed at one student. The one below, to a second student.

How long does his/her dinner last?
His/her dinner lasts ...

plate	bowl	knife	fork

spoon	chopsticks

We eat our food from a plate or a bowl. We eat our food with a knife, fork and spoon, or with chopsticks.

119

Make the action of eating from a plate.

What do we eat our food from?

We eat our food
from a plate or a bowl

What do we eat our food with?

We eat our food with a knife,
fork and spoon, or with chopsticks

 See Chart 7

many	more ... than	the most
few	fewer ... than	the fewest
much	more ... than	the most
little	less ... than	the least

| exception | quantity | singular |

"Many" and "much" have the same meaning, but we use "many" with things we can count. For example, we can count pens – one pen, two pens, three pens etc. We can count books, chairs etc. Generally, the things we can count have an "s" in the plural. "People" is an exception. It has no "s", but it is plural and we use "many" with it. For example, "There are many people in this town".

We use "much" with things we cannot count. For example, we cannot count water or sugar. We cannot say "one water, two waters"; "one sugar, two sugars" etc. These things are a singular quantity and have no "s". Money is not an exception; we can count money, but we do not say "one money, two monies". We say "one pound, two pounds"; "one dollar, two dollars" etc.

What's the difference between "many" and "much"?

The difference between "many" and
"much" is that we use "many" with things we
can count, and "much" with things we can't count

Give me a sentence with "many" in it, please.

There are
many cars in a large city

Give me a sentence with "much" in it.

I do not put
much sugar in my tea

"Few" and "little" also have the same meaning, but we use "few" with things we can count, and "little" with things we cannot count.

What's the difference between "few" and "little"?

The difference between "few" and
"little" is that we use "few" with things we
can count and "little" with things we can't count

Give me a sentence with "few" in it, please.

There are
few tables in this school

Give me a sentence with "little" in it.

I drink little milk

many	few

Are there many pictures on these walls?

No, there
aren't many pictures on these
walls; there are few pictures on these walls

Are there few people in a large city?

No, there aren't few
people in a large city; there
are many people in a large city

 Students read Lesson 19 on page 99

much	little	a lot of

salt	pepper

We can use "much" in questions and negative sentences, but in positive sentences we generally use "a lot of". For example, we do not say "I eat much bread"; we say "I eat a lot of bread".

Do you drink much water?

Yes, I drink a lot of water

Do you drink little water?

No, I don't drink little water; I drink a lot of water

Do you eat little bread?

No, I don't eat little bread; I eat a lot of bread

Do you eat much salt?

No, I don't eat much salt; I eat little salt

Do you put much pepper on your plate?

No, I don't put much pepper on my plate; I put little pepper on my plate

fewer ... than   less ... than   bank

The difference between "fewer ... than" and "less ... than" is that we use "fewer ... than" with things we can count, and "less ... than" with things we cannot count. For example, "I have <u>fewer</u> thumbs than fingers. I drink <u>less</u> milk than water".

What's the difference between "fewer ... than" and "less ... than"?

The difference between "fewer ... than" and "less ... than" is that we use "fewer ... than" with things we can count, and "less ... than" with things we can't count

Give me a sentence with "fewer ... than" in it, please.

There are fewer pictures in this room than chairs

Give me a sentence with "less ... than" in it.

I eat less food than my brother

Are there more people in Europe than in Asia?

No, there aren't more people in Europe than in Asia; there are fewer people in Europe than in Asia

Do you drink more milk than water?

No, I don't drink more milk than water; I drink less milk than water

Have you got more money than the bank of England?

No, I haven't got more money
than the Bank of England; I've got
less money than the Bank of England

Do you eat more meat than bread?

No, I don't eat more meat
than bread; I eat less meat than bread

The word "less" these days is often used in place of the word "fewer", probably because it has only one syllable and is easier to say. People often say such things as "less books" or "less people". Also, there is the argument about whether one can say "fewer than me" instead of "fewer than I", the continuation of the sentence being "fewer than I have". Many educated people these days would in fact say "Mr Brown has less pencils than me" instead of "Mr Brown has fewer pencils than I". The, teacher, however, should not confuse the students with such irregularities.

LESSON 24

the fewest   **the least**   **the one**

The difference between "the fewest" and "the least" is the same as the difference between "fewer ... than" and "less ... than". We use "the fewest" with things we can count, whereas we use "the least" we use with things we cannot count. For example, "Of these three places, London, Cambridge and Greenwich, Greenwich has the fewest buildings", and "Of these three people, Mr Brown, Mr Smith and Mr Jones, Mr Jones drinks the least coffee".

What's the difference between "the fewest" and "the least"?

> The difference between "the fewest" and "the least" is that we use "the fewest" with things we can count, whereas we use "the least" with things we can't count

Give me a sentence with "the fewest" in it, please.

> In my family, my brother is the one who reads the fewest books

Give me a sentence with "the least" in it.

> In my family, my sister is the one who eats the least bread

Of these three books, has this book got the most pages?

> No, of these three books, this book hasn't got the most pages; it's got the fewest pages

Who eats the least food in your family?

> My ... eats the least food in my family

Who drinks the least coffee in your family?

> My ... drinks the least coffee in my family

Of these three foods, bread, meat and salt, do you eat salt the most?

No, of those three foods, bread, meat and salt, I don't eat salt the most; I eat it the least

Each time you say the word "salt", rub your finger and thumb together as if you were sprinkling salt on food.

Of these three drinks, water, milk and wine, do you drink wine the most?

No, of those three drinks, water, milk and wine, I don't drink wine the most; I drink it the least

opposite   next to

Stand to the side of the table with the students in front of you and say **I'm standing opposite you. The table is next to me**.

Who's sitting opposite you?

... is sitting opposite me

Who's sitting next to you?

... is sitting next to me

What can you see opposite this building?

I can see another building etc. opposite this building

work   rest   most people

On Sunday we generally rest, but from Monday to Friday most people work.

Do most people rest from Monday to Friday?

No, most people don't rest from Monday to Friday; they work

Do you think most people like working?

No, I don't think most people like working; I think they dislike working

Do you work at the weekend?

Yes, I work at the weekend
~ No, I don't work at the weekend

glass   wood

The window's made of glass. The table's made of wood.

What's the window made of?

The window's made of glass

Is the table made of plastic?

No, the table isn't made of plastic; it's made of wood

paper   stone

This book's made of paper. The wall of the house behind Mr and Mrs Brown is made of stone.

What's this book made of?

This (or that) book's made of paper

What's the wall of the house behind Mr and Mrs Brown made of?

The wall of the house behind Mr and Mrs Brown is made of stone

enough

I'm tall enough to touch that picture, but I'm not tall enough to touch the ceiling.

Do you speak English well?

No, I don't speak English well, but I speak it well enough

Are you tall enough to touch the ceiling?

No, I'm not tall enough to touch the ceiling; I'm too short

Are you short enough to stand under the table?

No, I'm not short enough to stand under the table; I'm too tall

Is my pocket large enough to put this book into?

No, your pocket isn't large enough
to put that book into; it's too small

 Students read Lesson 20 on page 103

 See Chart 1

that one   repeat

**Instead of saying "This pencil is black and that pencil is white", we can say "This pencil
is black and that <u>one</u> is white", without repeating the word "pencil".**

What colour's this pencil?   This pencil's black

What colour's that one?   That one's white

Which pencil's red?   This pencil's red

Which one's grey?   This one's grey

Which book's open?   This book's open

Which one's closed?   This one's closed

badly

Can you hear well with your fingers in your ears?

No, I can't hear well with
my fingers in my ears; I hear badly

Do you see badly?

Yes, I see badly ~ No, I don't see
badly; I see well

| Does this pen write badly? | No, this pen doesn't write badly; it writes well |

| Do you speak ... badly? | No, I don't speak ... badly; I speak it well |

Insert the name of the student's language in the above question.

telephone　　　　**mobile**　　　　**phone**

call　　　　**make a (phone) call**

| Is there a telephone in your family home? | Yes, there's a telephone in my family home ~ No, there isn't a telephone in my family home |

| Have you got a mobile (phone) in your pocket? | Yes, I've got a mobile (phone) in my pocket ~ No, I haven't got a mobile (phone) in my pocket |

| How many phone calls do you make a day? | I make about ... phone calls a day |

 *Dictation 9*

The difference/ between "any" and "some"/ is that we generally use "any"/ in questions and negative sentences,/ whereas we use "some"/ in the positive./ "Any" is non-specific./ "How many" is specific./Are there any books/ on the table?/ Yes, there are some./ How many books are there/ on the floor?/ There are none./ The present continuous/ we use for an action/ we are doing now./ For example,/ I am speaking English now./ About how many pages/ are there in this book?

 *Do Revision Exercise 5*

Pronunciation Chart

It is here that you should check the students' pronunciation by going through the following lists of words and sentences with them. It is important that the students have control over the basic sounds of English by the end of Stage 4, and preferably by the end of Stage 2. Otherwise, they will find it difficult to correct themselves later and, consequently, could carry the mistakes with them forever. The lists and sentences can be put up on a wall of the classroom for you to point at. Alternatively, you could just read from the lists below, getting the students to repeat after you. It is better, however, if you can point at the words and get the students to make the mistakes before hearing your correct version. Students should first pronounce the word, you should then give them the correct pronunciation, and they then repeat after you.

/ɪ/		/əʊ/		/ɜː/		/ʌ/	
this	/ðɪs/	no	/nəʊ/	first	/fɜːst/	front	/frʌnt/
it's	/ɪts/	coat	/kəʊt/	third	/θɜːd/	London	/'lʌndən/
is	/ɪz/	don't	/dəʊnt/	her	/hɜː/	coming	/kʌmɪŋ/
city	/'sɪti/	both	/bəʊθ/	person	/'pɜːsən/	country	/'kʌntri/
miss	/mɪs/	only	/'əʊnli/	word	/wɜːd/	mother	/'mʌðə/
in	/ɪn/	most	/məʊst/	verb	/vɜːb/	some	/sʌm/
difference	/'dɪfrəns/	home	/həʊm/	prefer	/prə'fɜː/	son	/sʌn/
still	/stɪl/			turn	/tɜːn/	money	/'mʌni/
difficult	/'dɪfɪkəlt/					month	/mʌnθ/
milk	/mɪlk/					love	/lʌv/
little	/'lɪtl/						

/æ/		/ɔː/		/ʊ/		/h/		other	
as	/æz/	all	/ɔːl/	look	/lʊk/	home	/həʊm/	a	/ə/
hat	/hæt/	more	/mɔː/	book	/bʊk/	hat	/hæt/	an	/æn/
have	/hæv/	door	/dɔː/			head	/hed/	what	/wɒt/
man	/mæn/	wall	/wɔːl/			hear	/hɪə/	the book	/ðə/
		call	/kɔːl/			her	/hɜː/	the eye	/ðiː/
								we're	/wɪə/
								answering	/'aːnsərɪŋ/
								or	/ɔː/
								fifth	/fɪfθ/

1) This is his city.

2) Oh, no; don't go home.

3) The third, thirteenth and thirty-third.

4) Send some money to London.

5) Have you got that hat?

6) There are doors in all the walls.

7) Look at the book.

8) Her hat is on his head.

At this point, do a complete revision of Stages 1 and 2.

Vocabulary Test

1)	side	21)	begin
2)	walk	22)	made of
3)	married	23)	it will be
4)	tell	24)	it was
5)	friend	25)	building
6)	smell	26)	fewer ... than
7)	by car	27)	knife
8)	kind	28)	south
9)	nothing	29)	much
10)	during	30)	child
11)	silver	31)	love
12)	bag	32)	meal
13)	gold	33)	less
14)	key	34)	the fewest
15)	think	35)	paper
16)	instead of	36)	stone
17)	outside	37)	glass
18)	do	38)	wood
19)	many	39)	badly
20)	end	40)	plate

 *Dictation*

There are about/ thirty pages in that book./ He doesn't go home/ after the lesson./ They don't speak French, but English./ Are there any pictures/ on these walls?/ Yes, there are some./ I'm not asking or answering/ a question,/ but I'm reading a book./ We use "tall" and "short" for people,/ but "high" and "low" for things./ Who is coming to you?/ She's putting her finger/ into her mouth./ We've got four hands/ and two heads./ Their eyes are blue,/ but their hair is brown./ Is that right?/ No, it is wrong./ This part of my body/ is my foot.

Demonstration Charts

Chart 1

Chart 1

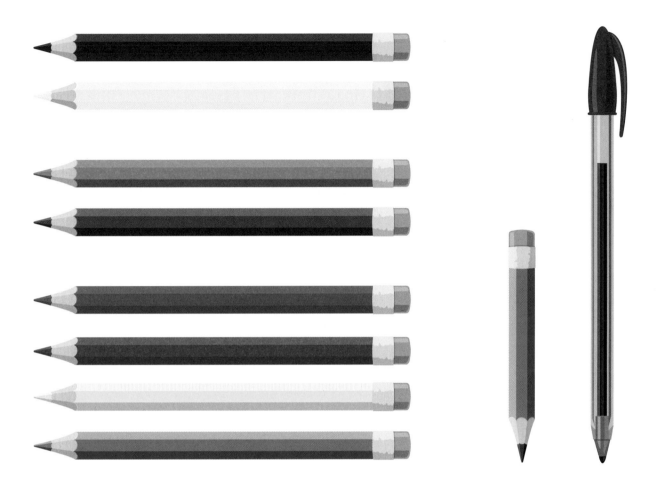

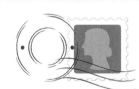

Dear John,

I'm having a good
time here.

See you soon.

Lots of love, Maria

John Brown,

Berwick House,

139 Oxford Street,

London W1D 2JA

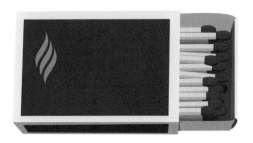

Chart 2

1	2	3	4	5	6	7
Aa	Bb	Cc	Dd	Ee	Ff	Gg

14	15	16	17	18	19	20
Nn	Oo	Pp	Qq	Rr	Ss	Tt

a e i o u

Verbs are words

What colour is the book?

a book

the book

Chart 2

8	9	10	11	12	13
Hh	Ii	Jj	Kk	Ll	Mm

21	22	23	24	25	26
Uu	Vv	Ww	Xx	Yy	Zz

? . , : ;

we use for actions.

The book is blue

an umbrella

the umbrella

Chart 3

13	30
14	40
15	50
16	60
17	70
18	80
19	90
20	100
	1,000
	1,000,000

Chart 3

313

1,815

1,950,630

$$2 + 2 = 4$$

$$\underline{1} \times 5 = 5$$

$$\underline{2} \times 5 = 10$$

$$\underline{3} \times \underline{5} = 15$$

$$\underline{4} \times \underline{5} = 20$$

$$
\begin{array}{r}
13 \\
+30 \\
\hline
43
\end{array}
$$

$$
\begin{array}{r}
15 \\
+50 \\
\hline
65
\end{array}
$$

Chart 4

non-specific

Any?

specific

How many?

non-specific

Anybody?

specific

Who?

non-specific

Anything?

specific

What?

Chart 4

Yes, some
No, not any

Seven etc.
None

Yes, somebody
No, not anybody

Mrs Brown etc.
Nobody

Yes, something
No, not anything

A light etc.
Nothing

Chart 5

Present continuous – now

Positive

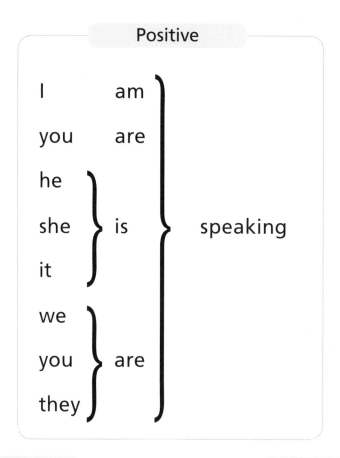

I	am	
you	are	
he		
she	is	speaking
it		
we		
you	are	
they		

Negative

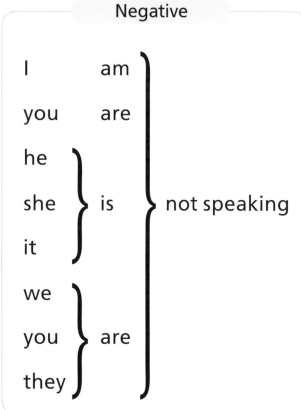

I	am	
you	are	
he		
she	is	not speaking
it		
we		
you	are	
they		

Questions

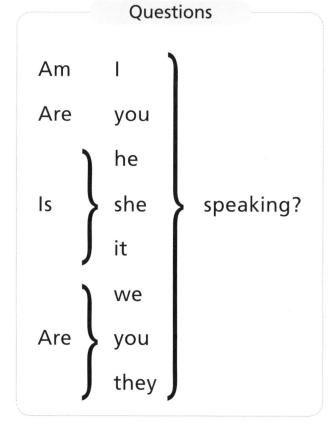

Am	I	
Are	you	
	he	
Is	she	speaking?
	it	
	we	
Are	you	
	they	

Chart 5

Present simple – generally

Positive

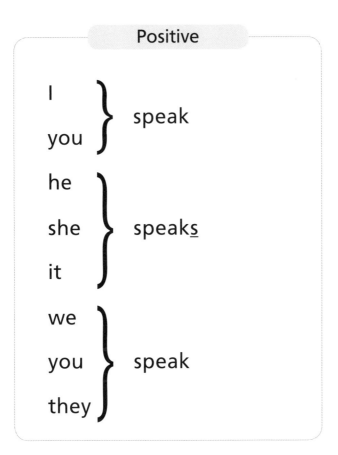

I
you } speak

he
she } speak<u>s</u>
it

we
you } speak
they

Negative

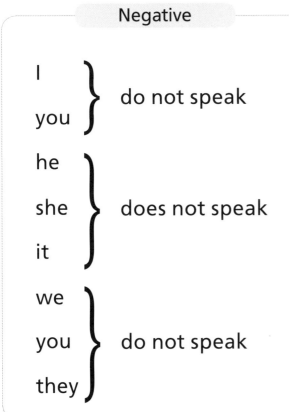

I
you } do not speak

he
she } does not speak
it

we
you } do not speak
they

Questions

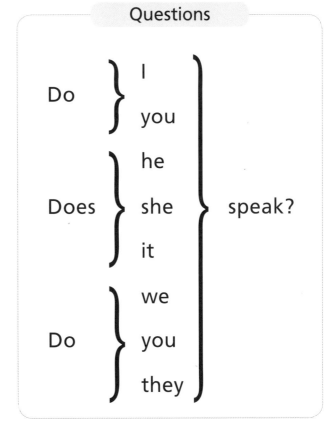

Do } I
you

Does } he
she } speak?
it

Do } we
you
they

Chart 6

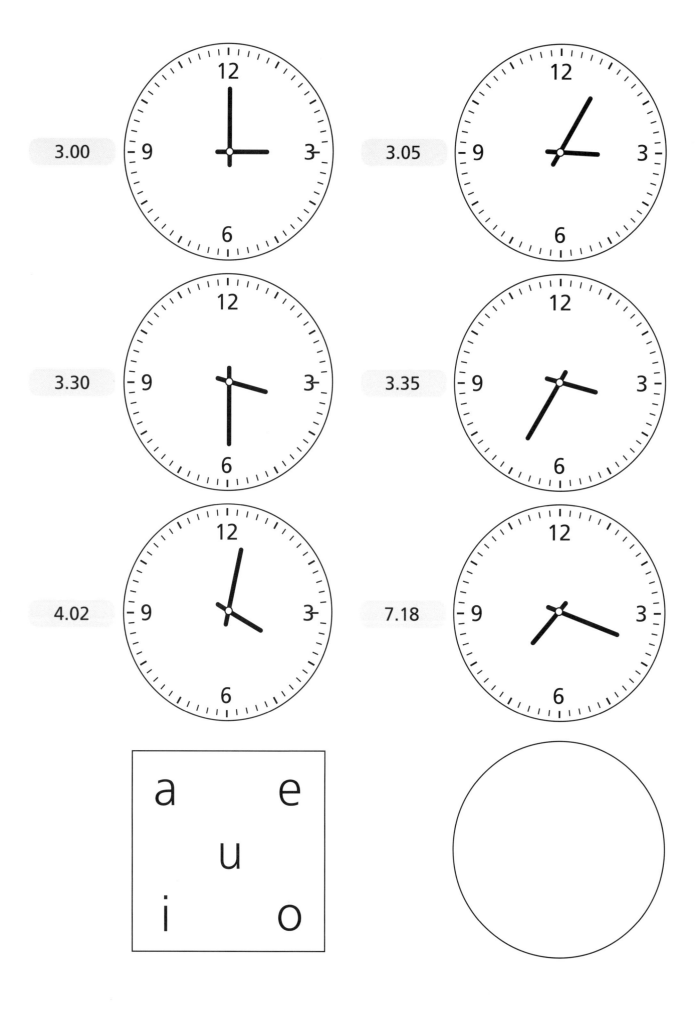

Chart 6

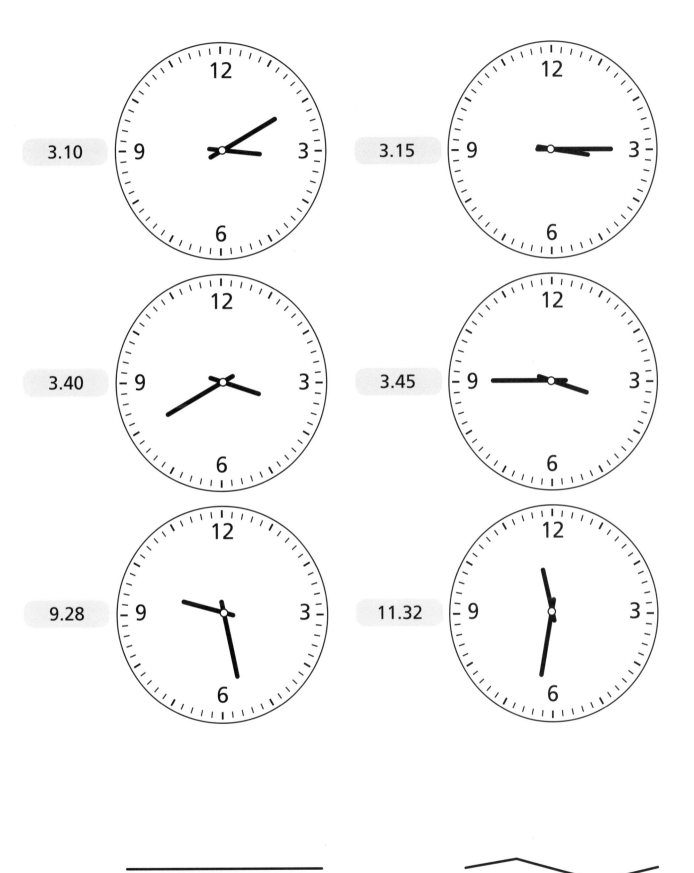

Chart 7

PLURAL — NUMBER —

many	—	more ... than —
few	—	fewer ... than —

SINGULAR — QUANTITY —

much	—	more ... than —
little	—	less ... than —

Chart 7

THINGS WE CAN COUNT

the most

the fewest

books

pens

people

THINGS WE CAN'T COUNT

the most

the least

water

sugar

money

Index

Notes

Notes

Notes

Notes

Notes

Notes

Notes